Praise for
The Grieving Student

"Specific, step-by-step guidance for facilitating healthy grief, avoiding development of problems, and treating grief that is complicated. . . . If there were just one book I would recommend to the teachers of my children, this absolutely would be it."
—Therese A. Rando, Ph.D., BCETS, BCBT
Clinical Director, The Institute for the Study and Treatment of Loss
Warwick, Rhode Island
Author, *Treatment of Complicated Mourning*

"All school personnel should be familiar with the basics put forth in this book. It provides a forum for meaningful dialogue and learning among students, teachers, and families. If a resource like this were available after the tragic events of September 11, 2001, I would have sent a copy to each of New York City's 1,000 schools and structured staff development efforts around the main themes of the book. This would have provided additional supports to help our children, teachers and families cope with the traumatic personal loss."
—Vincent Giordano, M.S.
Former Executive Director of the Division of Student Support Services
New York City Department of Education

"If only this book could be required reading for all teacher training programs! So many children and teens impacted by the death of a family member or close friend experience additional difficulties in the school setting, not because people don't care, but often because they simply do not know how to respond. This is a thorough, practical, and insightful guide for teachers new and seasoned, who find themselves unsure of what to do when death affects a student or students."
—Donna L. Schuurman, Ed.D., FT
Executive Director, The Dougy Center for Grieving Children & Families
Portland, Oregon

"This is a 'must-read' for any teacher! Through clear and concise writing and vignettes that bring the points home, this guide gives teachers essential information for understanding and supporting their students after a loss. This unique resource tackles a challenging topic and provides strategies for helping students cope and successfully return to the classroom."
—Robin H. Gurwitch, Ph.D.
Professor, Division of Developmental and Behavioral Pediatrics
Program Coordinator, National Center for School Crisis and Bereavement
Cincinnati, Ohio

"Provides a window into the personal experience of the bereaved child and offers practical and easy to follow strategies that teachers and schools can immediately utilize."

—**Thomas Demaria, Ph.D.**
Director, Psychological Services Center and 9/11 Family Center
Doctoral Program in Clinical Psychology, Long Island University

"Death is a part of life in K–12 schools. This wise book promotes understanding and provides practical guidelines that will support educators making this a time of learning and healing as well as grief for students and staff.

—**Jonathan Cohen, Ph.D.**
President, Center for Social and Emotional Education
Co-chair, National School Climate Council

"An indispensable and easy to read resource . . . written with compassion for the students and their families, as well as sensitivity to the very nature of grief and bereavement."

—**Duane M. Isava, Ph.D., NCSP**
Psychology Associate, Arundel Psychological Associates

"All students experience some sort of loss such as death or illness, but not all teachers and other educators know how to help them and their families through their grief. This book is an invaluable guide through the process and should be on every teacher's desk and in every school library."

—**Ralph E. (Gene) Cash, Ph.D., NCSP**
Florida Licensed Psychologist
Associate Professor, Center for Psychological Studies
Nova Southeastern University, Fort Lauderdale, Florida

"Will serve as a long-standing resource for educators who confront the confounding experience of children's grief. Reassuring guidance is combined with suggestions that can ease a child's pain and help return a child to learning in the classroom."

—**Marleen Wong, Ph.D., LCSW**
Assistant Dean and Clinical Professor
Director of Field Education, School of Social Work
University of Southern California

"The authors once again establish the important role teachers play in helping students find meaning in their lives . . . each suggested strategy can be used to help students acquire the cognitive skills and emotional regulation required to grapple with life's big questions."

—**Susan Craig, Ph.D.**
AGH Associates, Inc.
Hampton, New Hampshire

THE Grieving
Student

THE Grieving Student

A Teacher's Guide

by

David J. Schonfeld, M.D.
National Center for School Crisis and Bereavement
Division of Developmental and Behavioral Pediatrics
Cincinnati Children's Hospital Medical Center, Ohio

and

Marcia Quackenbush, M.S., MFT, CHES
ETR Associates
Scotts Valley, California

·P A U L·H·
BROOKES
PUBLISHING Co. ®

Baltimore • London • Sydney

Paul H. Brookes Publishing Co.
Post Office Box 10624
Baltimore, Maryland 21285-0624
USA
www.brookespublishing.com

"Paul H. Brookes Publishing Co." is a registered trademark of
Paul H. Brookes Publishing Co., Inc.

Typeset by Broad Books, Baltimore, Maryland.
Manufactured in the United States of America by
Versa Press, Inc., East Peoria, Illinois.

The individuals described in this book are either real or composites of real people whose situations are masked and are based on the authors' experiences. In all instances, names and identifying details have been changed to protect confidentiality.

Library of Congress Cataloging-in-Publication Data

Schonfeld, David J., 1959–
    The grieving student : a teacher's guide / by David J. Schonfeld and Marcia Quackenbush.
     p.   cm.
    Includes bibliographical references and index.
    ISBN-13: 978-1-59857-116-5 (pbk.)
    ISBN-10: 1-59857-116-8 (pbk.)
    1. Grief in adolescence.   2. Grief in children.   3. Teacher-student relationships.
I. Quackenbush, Marcia. II. Title.
BF724.3.G73S37 2010
155.9'37083—dc22   2010018036

British Library Cataloguing in Publication data are available from the British Library.

2014   2013   2012   2011   2010

10   9   8   7   6   5   4   3   2   1

Contents

About the Authors

David J. Schonfeld, M.D., Director, National Center for School Crisis and Bereavement (NCSCB) and Director, Division of Developmental and Behavioral Pediatrics, Cincinnati Children's Hospital Medical Center, has provided consultation, technical assistance, and training in the areas of pediatric bereavement and school crisis preparedness and response for more than 20 years. He has provided presentations at national and international meetings and worked with communities throughout the United States and abroad (including Europe, Great Britain, Asia, the Middle East, Scandinavia, Latin America, and Africa). In 1991, Dr. Schonfeld established the School Crisis Response Program at Yale University School of Medicine, where he provided training to tens of thousands of school-based personnel throughout the country and technical assistance in hundreds of school crisis events. Dr. Schonfeld has consulted with schools during the aftermath of numerous school (including school shootings and other school violence) and national crisis events. From 2001 to 2004, he consulted to the New York City Department of Education and coordinated training for school crisis teams in the wake of the September 11, 2001, terrorist attacks and provided training to more than 1,000 district- and school-level crisis teams within the system. In 2005, Dr. Schonfeld was awarded funding by the September 11th Children's Fund and the National Philanthropic Trust to establish the NCSCB. Dr. Schonfeld has worked with schools coping with large-scale natural disasters, such as Hurricane Katrina in New Orleans in 2005; Hurricane Ike in Galveston, Texas, in 2008; and the 2008 earthquake in Sichuan, China. Dr. Schonfeld is currently a member of the National Commission on Children and Disasters, the Disaster Mental Health Subcommittee of the National Biodefense Science Board, and the American Academy of Pediatrics's Disaster Preparedness Advisory Council. He is actively engaged in school-based research involving children's understanding of and adjustment to serious illness and death and school-based interventions to promote adjustment and risk prevention.

Marcia Quackenbush, M.S., MFT, CHES, Senior Editor and Health Education Specialist, ETR Associates, Scotts Valley, California, is a licensed family therapist and certified health education specialist. She has more than 15 years of clinical mental health experience, much of which is focused on children, adolescents, and families of people living with life-changing condition; or people coping with terminal illness in themselves or family members. Ms. Quackenbush has written extensively in the health education field, publishing numerous articles and books on a range of topics.

About the National Center for School Crisis and Bereavement
The NCSCB was founded in 2005 with generous support from the September 11th Children's Fund and the National Philanthropic Trust. It has provided support services to schools across the country. The goals of the NCSCB are to promote an appreciation of the role schools can serve to support students, staff, and families at times of crisis and loss; to link efforts to provide trauma-related and bereavement support services within school settings; to collaborate with professional organizations, governmental and nongovernmental agencies, and community groups to further these goals; and to serve as a resource for information, training materials, consultation, and technical assistance. Learn more at http://www.cincinnatichildrens.org/svc/alpha/s/school-crisis.

Foreword

"Kids are resilient; they'll get over this in no time." This phrase is repeatedly used as a statement of fact, an offer of reassurance, or even as a message of condolence. And it is true in part; most children possess an amazing ability to be resilient—to be able to return to a purposeful, functional life after the death of a loved one. But being resilient does not equate to an escape from the grief, sadness, fear, anger, and loss that are also associated with death. For a child, to be resilient is concurrently a blessing and a curse. Once a child returns to classwork or after-school sports, society attaches to him or her the label of *healed, moved on,* or *"over it,"* and he or she is left to walk the journey through grief alone.

Walking the journey alone is exactly what Dr. Schonfeld and Marcia Quackenbush seek to prevent through this excellent resource on childhood bereavement, *The Grieving Student: A Teacher's Guide.* They successfully remedy misunderstanding and discomfort—the largest obstacles between teachers and grieving students. Death is a difficult topic to confront; no one wants to talk about death or address a student in such a way as to exacerbate his or her sadness. As a result, teachers sometimes prefer to interact minimally to prevent doing or saying something "wrong." This can relay the message to a grieving student that no one cares at school, yet there is nothing further from the truth. Despite the fact that death is one of the few constants in life, there is a dramatic absence of professional development for educators in childhood bereavement. It is a present-day dilemma: Teachers do not know how to support a grieving child, yet the child in grief needs help. *The Grieving Student: A Teacher's Guide* does an exceptional job of filling this need.

I have some firsthand knowledge in this area. My husband was killed in the terrorist attacks of September 11, 2001. My children were only 6, 4, and 2 at the time. My youngest did not even understand death; my oldest struggled with fear. Yet they returned to school and play and even smiles soon after. It is nearly 9 years after this tragedy, and despite appearances and successes and teachers' assumptions, my children are not "over" their father's death. As they grow, there is more they comprehend about the horrific nature of how their dad died. There are more experiences they miss that only growing up can bring, such as father–daughter dances or father–son camp-outs; and important experiences that they cannot share with their father, such as graduations, scoring a first touchdown, or making the honor roll in high school. They experience loss frequently, but this burden they carry is overlooked by most of society.

Two years after September 11, 2001, my son began to exhibit anxiety related to his father's death. When discussing with his teacher how this was affecting his schoolwork, she queried, "It's been 2 years since his father died; isn't he over it yet?" While this comment sounds painfully harsh and unfeeling, it is actually an accurate representation of the misperception people have regarding children and loss. Once a grieving child begins to exhibit resilient behaviors, or after the passage of months, the child is presumed "over" the death of the loved one. As a result, declining social or academic performance that can be related to continuing grief is often attributed to something else, or punished as bad behavior.

It is necessary that educators understand the long-term consequences of a death experienced in childhood. One cannot teach a child unless he or she is available emotionally to learn. *The Grieving Student: A Teacher's Guide* also helps educators understand how grief might manifest over time. The authors remind teachers that "the loss of a family member or friend is an experience that never fully leaves a person. In many ways, deep losses stay with us throughout our lives," and they offer guidance on how to deal with these issues in the classroom most effectively.

Kids' grief is different from that of adults. They may seem to adapt to their grief more proficiently, but they often experience their loss in some capacity through the length of their childhood and development. They need support and understanding from those whose care they are in. Dr. Schonfeld and Ms. Quackenbush, with clear explanations and insightful case studies, provide the tools that educators need.

As a parent of three children who are well adjusted and amazingly resilient but who will always mourn in some capacity the loss of their father, this book is a welcome and much needed resource. It is an exceptional guide that will help teachers better demonstrate the care and concern they feel toward the grieving students who need their support the most. If it were up to me, this book would be mandatory reading for all of those in whose care we place our children who are forced to walk a journey through grief.

MaryEllen Salamone, PT, J.D.
Families of September 11 Advisory Board Member

Preface

In the late 1980s, early on in my fellowship training in developmental-behavioral pediatrics, a request was received from a local Catholic elementary school for someone to come and speak to the students. Three children had experienced deaths of family members from separate and unrelated natural causes, and the school thought it would be helpful for someone to talk to those students and their classmates. Although I had no prior experience in this area, I volunteered to go and talk with the class.

By the time I arrived a week later, the school was eagerly waiting. They brought the students together in the auditorium for an assembly and invited parents, teachers, the nuns, and school administrators to attend. The day ended with my meeting a member of the media so that other schools could learn of this "model program." I was impressed with the openness of the students and the warm environment that the school had created to help children cope with this important topic. I felt that I was able to join the school to do something important for these children that day (and learned never to try to do it as an assembly again).

Apparently, they found it helpful as well. I continued to be called to other schools throughout the city when there were deaths of students and staff. I was surprised to see how frequently these tragic incidents occurred. Families were referred to me to counsel their grieving children. Even faculty sought my advice on their own patients and schools where they were working. All along, all I could think was "Doesn't everyone else know how to do this?" Certainly, any adult knows more about why people die than the average kindergartner. Why don't they just listen to children who are grieving, answer the children's questions the best they can, and provide them with basic support?

During my fellowship, I wrote my first article, on the topic of how pediatricians can help schools by providing consultation around deaths of members of the school community. It was perhaps the only paper that has been accepted without a request for revision. The editor published it along with a simple message:

> Dr. Schonfeld's article is a most interesting and dedicated piece of writing. It describes, with remarkable insights, a new and important role for community and behaviorally oriented pediatricians. Most would not consider ourselves as consultants for these issues, but we probably can address them more comprehensively than any other professional group.[1]

What struck me the most from the comment was that most pediatricians would not consider themselves experts on this topic—but probably should. I decided that I should devote part of my career to convincing them just that.

As I planned to leave for my first faculty position at Yale University School of Medicine, I asked the city school system what I could do to thank them for the privilege of working with their students and staff. They asked me to train their staff to do what I had been doing for them for the past couple of years. It forced me to think of exactly what that was. I pulled together the mental health staff from the city school system and provided training in school crisis response and then published an article on a model to do just that. I have been doing school crisis work ever since.

Shortly after I started at Yale, a meeting was called to discuss how schools and other community groups could help children cope with our involvement in the Persian Gulf War of 1990–1991. By the time the meeting was held this war had ended, but we met anyway. The school representatives politely pointed out that the major cause of traumatic losses among their students was not the war, but rather the violent deaths of children at the hands of other children. They wanted advice on how to help children cope with these tragic events. From that meeting arose the School Crisis Prevention and Response Initiative, which involved educators, school administrators, mental health professionals, and law enforcement representatives. We developed a model for school crisis preparedness and response and provided training and consultation. We sought and received funding so that the program continued until I relocated to Cincinnati in 2005 and established the National Center for School Crisis and Bereavement (NCSCB) at Cincinnati Children's Hospital Medical Center.

Over the years, the program at Yale responded to hundreds of school crisis events and provided training to tens of thousands of school-related personnel, as well as other professional groups (including pediatricians and other pediatric healthcare providers). After the events of September 11, 2001, I was invited to oversee the training of school crisis response teams for New York City Public Schools. Within the first 18 months, along with a colleague, I provided more than 50 full-day training workshops for school crisis teams in all 41 school districts and approximately 1,000 schools within the system. At one point, several people came up to me after a workshop and simply said, "We think every teacher in the system should hear your presentation on bereavement—every teacher needs to know this." I asked how many teachers there were in NYC Public Schools. When they told me that it was more than 100,000, if you included paraprofessionals, I realized that there wasn't any way I could provide in-service training to all of them. I asked myself, "Why don't teachers learn this as part of their preservice education?" I decided then that part of my career would be devoted to trying to make that happen.

I have given many presentations across the United States and abroad. Invariably, people come up to me and ask, "Where can we get your book?" Although I have written many articles and book chapters on the topic for various professional groups, I hadn't yet written a book for teachers. If I was going to be true to my commitment to help every teacher become better prepared to help children who are grieving, then it was my responsibility to write this book.

In 2005, as mentioned, I was awarded generous support from the September 11th Children's Fund and the National Philanthropic Trust to establish the NCSCB at Cincinnati Children's Hospital Medical Center. One of our major goals is to elevate school staff's understanding of the impact of bereavement and trauma on the lives of children and the capacity of school personnel to provide much needed support. To do this, we seek to ensure that individuals training to become teachers or other school professionals will learn how to support grieving children as part of their preservice education. In-service training is also needed for our current educators and other school personnel (e.g., school mental health professionals, school administrators). This book is one step toward reaching that goal.

I turned to Marcia Quackenbush to help me write the book. We had coauthored elementary school AIDS and cancer education curricula many years ago, and she had served as a consultant on several federal research projects to assist with curriculum and teacher training materials. Knowledgeable herself about schools and how to support grieving children, above all she knew how to communicate this information in a voice that was readily accessible to teachers and other school personnel. I was thrilled when she agreed to coauthor this book and when Paul H. Brookes Publishing Co. indicated their interest in publishing it.

There are many people that I could thank for helping to teach me what I aim to share with you in this book. My own parents showed me firsthand how important it is to communicate openly and honestly with children. My wife, Joanne, and daughters, Kim and Sara, patiently demonstrated how much more difficult such communication is to accomplish—and helped me figure out how to do it better. Whether as young children, or now as young adults, my daughters have amazed me by their capacity to understand and deal with issues in remarkably mature ways (well, most of the time, at least). I like to believe it is in part because of the trust my wife and I have placed in them and our willingness to see this capacity and help them reach it. I am also grateful that my wife and daughters forgave me when I answered evening or weekend calls from parents and schools because, yes, they appreciated that these really were crises and understood the need for my travel away from home. It can be difficult working with grieving children and communities, and my wife and children were there to provide me with support and grounding when I returned home. Outside of my family, my mentors helped me learn what I know about the field and to hone my skills, and my colleagues within the NCSCB continue to answer the questions that I still have and to provide the professional support and camaraderie that allows me to continue in this work.

But perhaps I would like to thank the most those educators and their students who have given me the privilege to be with them in some of their most difficult times, who have allowed me to see their vulnerability and to witness their enormous strength and wisdom. People often ask how I can spend so much of my time being with individuals who are grieving. "It must be so depressing," they observe. Medical professionals wonder why I would work with families after it's already "too late to do anything." But I have found this work to be incredibly gratifying. You meet people and connect with them at a time when they are most in need of that personal connection and, ultimately, you are able to help them—not through the use of medications or technology—but because of your interpersonal skills and what you bring to the interaction as a person who genuinely cares and really wants and is able to help.

As teachers and other school staff, you have the opportunity to help your students every day. Although school crisis events are relatively rare, they tend to dominate the news. It may be all that people think of when the topic of bereavement in schools is discussed, which is in and of itself quite rarely. But what really matters is the help that you provide day-to-day to individual children who are struggling to understand and cope with the death of a family member or friend. It is often at a time when few, if any, are willing to provide that support or even think they are able to. Some teachers and other school professionals rise to the occasion and provide education and support that is literally life-changing for these grieving children. It may not be newsworthy, but it can mean the world to them.

After you have read this book, I hope you will find that although you, too, may not have considered yourself as someone to address these issues, you probably can address them more comprehensively than any other professional group. My hope is that you will allow yourself to reach out a little more than you may have in the past to students and families and provide just a bit more support to help grieving children heal a little faster.

I thank you for the work that you do every day and for the opportunity to contribute to it.

David J. Schonfeld, M.D.

ENDNOTE

1. Schonfeld, D. (1989). Crisis intervention for bereavement support: A model of intervention in the children's school. *Clinical Pediatrics, 28*(1), 27–33.

Acknowledgments

The authors would like to acknowledge the generous support of the September 11th Children's Fund and the National Philanthropic Trust, which allowed for the establishment of the National Center for School Crisis and Bereavement in 2005. They have provided the majority of the support for the work of the NCSCB; this book would likely not have been written without their financial and personal support and commitment.

Introduction

Yes, This Matters

If you're reading this book, chances are you're a teacher or someone else who works with children and young people. Like most other adults, you've probably experienced the death of a loved one at some point in your life—a friend; a classmate; or perhaps a parent, sibling, spouse, or other family member. You understand that these losses can have powerful and sometimes surprising effects, and that the process of grieving takes time and patience.

Children* also experience a range of significant losses. How common are these losses? They appear to be virtually universal. Before they reach adulthood, almost all children will experience the death of someone important to them. Approximately 5% will face the death of a parent by age 16.[1] Many will confront other deaths that affect them deeply—of siblings, friends, grandparents, beloved aunts or uncles, close family friends, or teachers. We all understand that the death of a parent is a profound loss for most children. It's important to recognize, however, that any of these deaths is likely to be difficult.

A recent study surveyed more than 8,000 students in Grades 4–12 attending New York City public schools.[2] The study was conducted 6 months after the terrorist attacks of September 11, 2001, but included questions about experiences of the students *before* 9/11. Thirty-nine percent had seen someone killed or seriously injured prior to the attacks. Almost a third (29%) had experienced the violent or accidental death of a close friend. More than 1 in 4 (27%) had experienced the violent or accidental death of a family member.

Of note, a comparable study had looked at these same issues in Kansas back in 1978.[3] Researchers surveyed students attending two public high schools and found outcomes surprisingly similar to the 2002 New York study. Ninety percent of students reported having experienced the death of a grandparent, aunt, uncle, sibling, or someone else they cared about. Four in ten reported the death of a close friend their own age. Twenty percent had witnessed a death directly. These studies make it clear that the death of a friend or relative is a common experience for children.

Naturally, because we care about the welfare of children, we are concerned about the impact of these experiences. How do children make sense of such losses? What effect do these have on their schoolwork? On their personal adjustment? How wide is the arc of these deaths—are friends and classmates affected when a

---

*In this book, the term *children* refers to children of all ages, including teens, except when we mention a specific age.

student experiences the death of a friend or relative? What can schools and teachers do to help?

We have gotten answers to these questions through research, the clinical work of health and mental health providers, the experiences of teachers, and the work done through the NCSCB. It is quite clear to us that the effect of a death is felt deeply by children who are close relatives and friends and is often also felt by their classmates and friends. Although the death of a family member or friend is a common and normal event for children, it is also one that has a tremendous impact.

THE IMPACT OF DEATH ON CHILDREN

Here are some of the ways children are typically affected when they experience the death of a parent or other relative or friend:

- *Academics.* Children experiencing grief often find it difficult to concentrate. They may not be able to focus on reading, writing projects, or class discussions. They are easily distracted. Their academic performance and grades suffer.

- *Confusion.* The fact of the death and what it means often confuses children. The reactions of others can be upsetting or puzzling. What's expected of them may be unclear. Their own powerful feelings can be surprising and disconcerting.

- *Feelings and symptoms.* Depressed mood is common. Children may feel sad or anxious. They may have trouble with sleep, feel less alert, or experience outbursts of frustration or anger. They may become clingy or start to act younger and more childish. They may complain of headaches or stomachaches.

- *Guilt and shame.* Children often experience feelings of guilt or shame about the death.

- *Isolation.* Children usually feel isolated by these powerful experiences. They may not know how to communicate their thoughts and feelings to friends, teachers, or others.

- *Worsening of preexisting challenges.* Some children are already struggling with learning, social skills, or mental health challenges. The extra burden of grief usually worsens such preexisting conditions.

Friends and classmates may be confused about how to respond to a peer who has lost a relative or friend. What should they say or do? Who can they turn to for guidance? The death may bring up memories of an earlier loss they experienced themselves. They may feel resentful about or frustrated by the changes a friend goes through. Their own anxiety about the health and safety of their parents and family often increases—if this could happen to a friend, could it happen to them, too?

IT HELPS WHEN ADULTS AND CHILDREN TALK

One of the reasons adults may not realize how common experiences of loss are for children is because people simply don't have conversations about death very often. Many adults aren't especially comfortable talking about the subject. Most of us have little experience, and there aren't many models to follow.

When the topic of death comes up around children, a number of additional factors can complicate the conversation. To begin with, adults and children have different communication styles about the topic. Sometimes, they miss each other's signals. An adult doesn't realize a child is communicating about grief or death. Children may be confused about what adults are trying to say.

Fortunately, there are some straightforward principles and guidelines that allow teachers and others to communicate clearly with children and answer the questions they are likely to have. Helping children talk about and understand death and grief helps them cope more successfully with their lives.

Constructive conversations between adults and children help. Grieving students feel more connected and supported. They are likely to do better emotionally, socially, and academically. Students' families feel more confident that their children are getting appropriate support. Most often, families appreciate sharing the burden of these matters with teachers. Classmates feel more certain about steps they can take to respond to their friend. Teachers themselves are gratified that they can do something to help. This is empowering for everyone, and helps teachers feel less anxious about their student's welfare.

Common Barriers to Communication

Through our work at the NCSCB, one of the things we have learned most profoundly is that grieving children *need* the kind of information and support teachers can give. Communicating about death and grief helps them understand what has happened. They can get answers to their questions about why the person died, how the death might change their lives, or even what death means. Communication also helps them understand what will happen for them in the coming days, weeks, months, and years. This understanding is the first step in coping with these complex events.

Common barriers to communication between adults and children include the following:

- *Adults and children have different communication styles.* Adults tend to use words to communicate. Children often use play. Adults may speak symbolically about death. Young children are more concrete and often don't understand the symbolism. Adults have ideas about socially acceptable behaviors to communicate feelings of sadness and grief. Children may not yet have learned these rules or may follow rules accepted by their peers, and their behaviors and responses can be confusing to adults.

- *Death is often a taboo subject.* This is especially true for some families in some cultures. Sometimes, for example, it is improper to speak the name of the dead or talk about the details of a death. However, almost everyone feels a special weight in discussions of death. Most people don't have much experience talking about death. These things make it a difficult topic to address with anyone, including children.

- *Adults don't want to create fear or anxiety in a child or make a child upset.* Teachers and others naturally wonder if bringing up a death simply makes the feelings and consequences worse. As we will see, however, it is the death itself—not the conversation—that is upsetting to the child.

- *Adults may worry that such discussions will bring up their own anxiety.* Because we have limited experiences talking about death, we are not always certain what our own reactions will be as we talk to children.

- *Adults feel unprepared.* Most of us lack practice talking about death. We imagine children might feel just as unprepared as we are. We worry that we'll get ourselves into something we can't manage in a useful way.

- *It's difficult to keep trying.* It's not at all uncommon for first or second attempts at such discussions with children to feel "unsuccessful." A child may not respond as we expect, or may become upset. Children may brush off an attempt at communication. Adults don't want to keep trying if their efforts aren't really helping the situation.

- *Children worry about creating anxiety in adults.* Children know that these topics make adults anxious. They may have seen powerful expressions of grief among family members that confuse them. In the same way that adults hesitate to open up conversations that might cause distress in children, children act to protect the adults in their lives.

- *It's not the right time.* Another reason that both adults and children may avoid these conversations is because it may never quite feel like the right time. Children often worry that their teachers are too busy. They're not sure when it would be appropriate to bring up their concerns. Teachers may sense that a grieving child simply wants to apply him- or herself to the school tasks that await—just to be a regular kid in school.

Teachers may have other practical concerns, such as how to find the time to do this given busy classroom schedules, whether families will object, or what to do if a child appears to need more support than the teacher can offer.

TEACHERS CAN HELP STUDENTS

In this book, we provide guidelines that help teachers judge how and when to bring up the topic of death with a grieving child. We give specific examples of things a teacher can say. We address other common concerns, such as what to do if religious topics come up. We also suggest ways to integrate conversations about death into everyday classroom experiences using teachable moments and planned activities.

You'll see that these steps

- Don't need to take a lot of time
- Are not difficult to do
- Do make an important difference in children's lives
- Make your students' learning more efficient and successful

These efforts can give all students the language and tools to talk about death and strong feelings. Everyone should have the benefit of these basic skills that allow them to turn to others for support and understanding in times of need.

TEACHERS CAN HELP FAMILIES

In this book, we also provide advice on ways teachers can advise parents. Parents look to teachers as trusted authorities and as caring professionals who know a great deal about their children. Many parents are not sure what to do to help their children after the death of a family member or friend. Teachers often have opportunities to offer suggestions as they talk to parents about how their child is doing academically and socially in the school setting. This can be some of the most important advice families receive.

ABOUT THE STORIES

Throughout the book, we have used stories to illustrate experiences students and teachers have involving death and bereavement. Although the stories are based on true experiences, we have altered them for a few reasons: 1) to preserve confidentiality, 2) to make them briefer, and 3) to better illustrate a particular point. As a result, some of the specifics have been changed and some stories are actually composites. All of the individuals' names have been changed.

Some of the stories focus on schools and classrooms, but we have also included some that are more clinical, involving counselors or health care providers. The clinical stories highlight some of the ways death and grief affect children's school and social behaviors that may not be as evident to teachers in their classroom role. We think teachers will find this additional background understanding helpful.

MAKING A DIFFERENCE: THE DEATH OF A FRIEND

This essay was written by a 15-year-old student who lost a friend to suicide late one summer. It describes her experience returning to school at the start of the new year and powerfully expresses how important a contact from a teacher can be at such times. (In Chapters 5 and 6, we describe some specific ways teachers can approach students who have experienced the death of someone they care for.)

Solace or support during grief was something I found very little of at school. Despite school normally being a bustling haven of friends and intellect and business for me, it became a place of exhausting struggle after T took his life. I felt isolated and ignored almost all of the time. Every day I would watch hundreds of other students rush past me as if they were functioning at a much faster and more confusing pace. I became lost amidst maddeningly unaware, light-hearted teenagers and frighteningly speechless adults.

My mother sent me to school that fall with a note explaining that I was "dealing with the loss of a friend." I had one note and seven teachers—seven blank, uncomfortable stares as they read, and seven pairs of adult eyes ashamedly avoiding my gaze as they calmly handed my note back to me. What they didn't realize as they so quickly returned that small paper was that at the same time they were handing to me hard, undeniable evidence that someone had been taken from me, something incomprehensible had happened—something devastating and awful, recorded on paper as a mere fact devoid of emotion.

It was hard to let the testimony of my shattered world pass so irreverently from me, to people I hardly knew, and back to me again, with it staring me in the face the way they could not. The day of T's funeral I also ran into a gym teacher who had had a habit of saying to morose-looking students, "Be happy you woke up alive." That day he chose to bark his mantra at me. I have always known him as a kind, thoughtful man—and I still know him as that man—but now, out of habit, I avoid him.

However, I had one teacher, my algebra teacher, make a difference that day. He held out my mother's note to me and, as I tugged it back, he held fast, catching my eye, and said, "I am truly sorry." Mr. H., with just a solid, unwavering glance and a sincere apology, had begun my process back into the reality I had lost. My classmates and the ticking clock and whirring, harsh world were all still spinning at what seemed to be an almost violent speed. But someone had shown that he cared, and that meant all the difference. A former history teacher also stopped a friend of mine in the hallway—someone who had also known T—and mentioned that he knew she was going through a hard time. He didn't mean to bring up anything upsetting, but wanted to let her know that he was thinking of her.

Things like that—being stopped in the hallway and reminded you're in someone's thoughts, or a genuine smile, or especially a sincere condolence—make the distinction between a teacher and a mentor, an adult and a friend. Showing or reminding someone that you care has a profound effect at any time in his or her life. But the same display of care or concern during grief can mean so much. It provides connection and positive interaction when you have felt that there was none, and a reminder that you haven't completely lost what you used to have. There are people who miss your smile and see your pain and truly mourn your loss. Despite destruction and death and sadness, I am not alone—and I am thankful for the people who helped me realize that.

ENDNOTES

1. Mahon, M. (1993). Children's concept of death and sibling death from trauma. *Journal of Pediatric Nursing, 8*(5), 335–344.

2. Hoven, C., Duarte, C., Lucas, C., Wu, P., Mandell, D., & Goodwin, R., et al. (2005). Psychopathology among New York City public school children 6 months after September 11. *Archives of General Psychiatry, 62*(5), 545–552.
3. Ewalt P., & Perkins, L. (1979). The real experience of death among adolescents: An empirical study. *Social Casework, 60,* 547–551.

To my daughters, Kim and Sara,
who taught me to respect the capacity of children
to understand even difficult issues
and the value of taking the effort to help them comprehend
and cope with challenges in their lives

And to teachers everywhere,
who have the unequaled privilege to play this critical role
in the lives of so many children

1
Why Schools and Teachers?

Isn't This Someone Else's Job?

The emphasis of this book is to help students who are grieving. One of the most effective ways to do this is to help *all* children understand more about death as part of their ongoing learning about life. Virtually all students will, at some point, deal with the death of a family member or friend. Offering anticipatory guidance provides them with the understanding and resources that will allow them to cope better when such events occur, whether in their own lives or in those of friends or classmates.

Schools and teachers are an important influence in the lives of children. The relationship they have with children is distinct—different from families, neighbors, churches, or clubs. As we will point out, teachers are uniquely qualified to help students understand more about death. They can play an essential role in supporting children who are grieving.

SCHOOLS ARE A SUPPORTIVE ENVIRONMENT

Students look to teachers for support and guidance with a variety of issues. Teachers help children understand the academic elements of their world, such as how to do long division, choose a good topic for a report, or understand the steps in mitosis. Likewise, teachers are a resource to whom children naturally turn when they have questions about death.

Often, students who have concerns regarding death are more comfortable turning to a trusted teacher than to a school counselor or a mental health provider. Teachers can provide guidance without any suggestion that there is something "wrong" with a student. That is, students may feel that they can more easily approach a teacher than talk with a school counselor, who generally meets with troubled students. Similarly, families are frequently more comfortable receiving support and services in a school setting, which may not carry the same sort of stigma as mental health services.

The following are some reasons why schools are an excellent setting for children to learn more about death and how to cope with a loss:

- *Schools are familiar.* They provide a safe and known setting, which makes them ideal for learning more about topics that are unknown, even if those topics might evoke confusion or anxiety.

1

- *Schools offer a variety of trained staff.* Teachers can check with other teachers, administrators, school counselors, district mental health specialists, or others for guidance in addressing issues of death and grieving. Students can also be assisted directly by a range of these qualified, knowledgeable professionals.

- *Students spend a good deal of time at school.* There are many different opportunities during the school year to address death and related issues.

- *Large numbers of children can be served.* Schools remain the best setting in which to reach the largest number of children.

Schools are also a particularly effective environment for supporting children who are grieving. Teachers can often monitor these students more easily than counselors or other professionals because they have ongoing contact with them. They spend more time with them daily in a natural environment and are often more familiar with them personally.

A student's grief may exhibit itself in a variety of ways that emerge in school settings rather than at home. For example, a child may begin acting out, put less effort into lessons and homework, or have conflicts with classmates. Grieving students who find themselves unable to concentrate may become frustrated or anxious. Teachers may be able to compare how a student's behavior differs before and after a loss. They can also evaluate a student's behavior in light of the many other students they have taught. This gives them a strong basis of comparison, which helps them determine whether a child needs additional support or services.

Most of the time, families appreciate the additional support that teachers and schools can provide. They view teachers as reliable sources of information about their children. Grieving families may be too overwhelmed to see or accurately assess the effects of grief on their children. They respect teachers' expertise, and they look to them for advice at challenging times.

TEACHERS CAN BENEFIT FROM THEIR DISTANCE FROM THE LOSS

Schools and teachers must balance many demands during the school day. Classroom time is committed to required subjects and test preparation, which leaves little time for addressing other needs. Many teachers, however, feel they are being asked to act as social workers for troubled students. Some, quite reasonably, might ask, "Shouldn't families be taking on this role of helping children understand death and cope with grief?"

The answer, of course, is that families *do* need to give their children opportunities to understand life and death. When families have experienced a loss, their children will look first to them for emotional support. Families have a unique and essential role in helping children through these experiences. However, when a family is touched by a death, children also need support beyond the family. Children learn quickly that grief places burdens on family members. A child knows, for example, that if he talks with his mother about how much he misses his father, she will feel sad. Some parents, struggling with their own grief, simply cannot give their children full support. Even parents who are able to be emotionally present and supportive with their children cannot fulfill all the needs children have at such times.

Teachers, therefore, have something to offer that families cannot—distance from the loss. In most instances, a teacher is not as personally involved in the death, even though the child's questions may bring up sadness and reflection for a teacher, and even personal memories of loss. Children experience an immediate quality of personal grief, however, that is part of their interactions with family members after the death of a family member or family friend. This is not part of their communication with a teacher. It can be an immense relief for children to ask their questions and seek support without feeling that they have to protect the teacher. This distance—in addition to teachers' understanding of developmental issues, their familiarity with students' day-to-day behavior, and their experiences responding to children's questions and needs—makes it clear how powerful teacher support can be.

UNDERSTANDING WHAT TO DO

The introduction to this book acknowledges that death *is* a challenging topic. Teachers may feel apprehensive about having conversations with students concerning death for valid reasons. The same strategies and skills that allow teachers to be effective in other areas of teaching, however, work very well when talking with children about death and grief. These strategies include having a basic understanding of the topic and a framework for addressing the subject in ways that make sense to students. This book provides both. The information here allows teachers to address issues relevant to children's understanding about death and apply strategies that fit their own approaches to teaching.

Often, these interventions can be quite brief. In most cases, supporting grieving children and helping all students learn more about death provides impressive benefits with a very modest investment of time. To do this well, however, teachers need to understand more about how children understand death, how to talk to them about it, and how to determine what to do if a grieving child is having problems.

Why should teachers make these efforts? For the same reason they do everything they do—because good teachers don't just teach the basics, they make a difference in children's lives.

LAYING THE GROUNDWORK: HELPING ALL STUDENTS

The foundation of helping children understand death begins with all students, not just grieving students. Teachers can use three approaches: 1) planned coursework, 2) teachable moments at the class level, and 3) teachable moments with individuals or small groups, to help all students gain a better understanding about death.

These approaches give students opportunities to address misconceptions and gain a greater understanding of the topic. What they learn in these exchanges will help them at any point in the future when they experience the death of a family member or friend. They can also help them make sense of a death they may have already experienced. Finally, they help children be better supports to friends and classmates who are experiencing a loss.

Planned Coursework

Some classes may have lessons in place that specifically address issues of life and death.[1] Some may address emotions, such as sadness, grief, happiness, and anger. This sort of coursework might be a part of a health education program or social development and life skills class. Older students might address these issues in a psychology or comparative religions class.

A Classmate's Help

A kindergarten class had talked about what it means when someone dies. Students discussed times when they had been sad, and they shared ideas about things they could do when they had sad feelings. Suggestions included talking with their parents or a friend. Some said that drawing a picture made them feel better. Some liked to play with their pets.

A few days after one of these lessons, the teacher overheard one of her students, Misha, talking with Liza, a child from the other kindergarten class. Liza said she was feeling very sad because her grandmother had recently died. Misha said, "I'm sorry. Maybe you would like to draw a picture of your grandma. We learned that can help you feel better."

Teachable Moments at the Class Level

Teachable moments that can address death will come up in most classes at some point. History and current events often involve issues of death and loss. Local events, such as a natural disaster (e.g., flood, earthquake, fire), often involve deaths that students want to talk about. Celebrities known to students may die or become seriously ill or injured, which may raise anxiety and concern in students. In addition, it is common for elementary classes to have a class pet, such as a fish or a turtle, that may die, which will have an effect on the students.

The Hamster Died

One Monday morning, students in a sixth-grade science class were surprised to discover that the hamster in the cage at the back of the classroom had died over the weekend. The animal hadn't really been a pet; in fact, it belonged to one of the other classes. No one in the class expressed any strong feelings of sadness.

One of the boys, however, looked at the curled body and said, "Look! He was going to the bathroom when he died. Yuck!" All of the students crowded around the cage to stare, joke, push each other, and laugh about this strange indignity. Their teacher called for order, got them to their seats, and matter-of-factly began to describe some of the physiological processes of death. He described several features that were evident in the body of the hamster, including the relaxation of the sphincter muscles, which might result in excretion of feces.

After their initial display of anxiety and discomfort, the students settled down, listened to their teacher, and asked a number of honest and thoughtful questions about biology and death. It became an instructive morning for the class.

Teachable Moments with Individual Students or Small Groups

Interactions related to attitudes or understanding of death may occur on the playground, in small groups working on a class project together, or among friends. For example, children may tease one another, challenge beliefs or experiences, or provide misinformation to one another. Teachers who observe these exchanges can use the opportunity to provide clarification and guidance.

Unruly in Line

A group of fifth graders stood in line at one of the playground games during recess. Two of the girls began a commotion. "You're dead," said Mariah as she pushed the other.

"No, you're dead," Felicia replied, pushing back.

Both girls were smiling and seemed playful as they did this. They continued to push each other, however, and both the taunts and the pushing became fiercer. The other students, annoyed at being shoved out of place themselves, started pushing and shouting back. From across the playground, their teacher saw her usually well-behaved students in an unruly process of shoving and shouting. She heard one of the boys call, "*You* guys are so dead."

"You're dead, you're dead," said another.

"No, you're all dead," Mariah called back.

"Stop it. This isn't funny," another student cried.

"Please stop," the teacher called as she approached the group. She waited until they calmed down, and then asked, "What is going on here?"

All of the students spoke at once with descriptions, defenses, and accusations. The teacher stopped them and asked them to talk about how they felt about the words that were being used. Several students mentioned being disturbed by the taunting and repetitions about death. The group became more serious, and everyone seemed willing to acknowledge that this kind of play had been hurtful. Mariah and Felicia became quite contrite and apologized to the group.

Later that day, the teacher spoke with the two of them privately. She talked with them about the seriousness of death and mentioned some of the feelings people often have when they lose someone they care about. She asked directly if either of them was going through a loss. Neither indicated anything troubling going on in their own lives. Their teacher knew, however, that their relationship could occasionally become aggressive.

The teacher explained that it was not possible for them to know if people around them had gone through the death of a loved one. Their teasing could be hurtful in ways they probably didn't realize. They agreed that they had not meant to upset their classmates.

The three of them talked about better ways Mariah and Felicia could deal with each other's teasing in the future, and both seemed willing to speak with her if they had problems. Their apologies seemed genuine, and they agreed to avoid future disturbances on the playground.

BEING READY: SETTING THE STAGE

Teachers can use the fairly simple steps of planned coursework and teachable moments at the class, small group, or individual level to help children better understand death and cope with the loss of a loved one. These interventions *are* important. Children have questions about death. Taking time to help them understand death and grief clarifies misconceptions and reduces anxiety, which promotes better academic achievement.

When teachers and students are able to have these conversations, teachers will find it easier to approach a bereaved child. This can also help prevent or minimize some of the common difficulties grieving children have, such as having trouble concentrating, becoming disruptive in class, or becoming isolated.

When bereaved children receive support outside of their home, they are more likely to navigate the entire grief process with less difficulty. Although each child will experience this support differently, it can help children achieve such things as positive emotional health, the ability to maintain strong social connections and contribute to their community, and the satisfaction of enjoying a rewarding life as an adult.

ENDNOTE

1. For a research study demonstrating that school-based lessons can advance young children's understanding of concepts related to death, see Schonfeld and Kappelman (1990).

2

How Children Understand Death

When a death occurs, children share many of the same experiences as adults, but their understanding of what they mean may be different. Teachers and other adults can help children understand death accurately. This involves more than simply giving them the facts, however. It also means helping them grasp some important concepts.

Adult support allows children to achieve a more complete understanding of death so that children may view death more realistically and with less anxiety. It helps grieving children adjust to their loss as they continue to move forward in their lives.

FOUR BASIC CONCEPTS ABOUT DEATH

Some discussions about children's understanding of death draw upon an ages and stages model. However, there is wide variation in the ways children of the same age understand death based on what they have experienced and what they already know about it. In general, most children will learn the four basic concepts discussed here by 5–7 years of age;[1,2] however, when personal experience is supported by thoughtful explanations and knowledge provided by teachers, children several years younger often come to understand these concepts as well.[3]

Everyone, including children, must understand the Four Concepts About Death to fully grieve and come to terms with a death.[4,5,6,7] Similar to young children, teens and adults often struggle with accepting the reality of a death. Intellectually, they may have a full and rational understanding, but emotionally they often find it difficult to accept what they know to be true. Children who do not yet understand these basic concepts are at a marked disadvantage. They cannot begin to accept something they do not yet understand.

It is best not to assume that children know certain things about death based on their age. Instead, teachers can ask them to talk about their ideas, thoughts, and feelings. As they explain what they already understand about death, what they still need to learn becomes evident.

Concept 1: Death Is Irreversible

In cartoons, television shows, and movies, children may see characters "die" and then come back to life. In real life, this is not going to happen. Children who do not fully understand this concept may view death as a kind of temporary separation. They often think of people who have died as being far away, perhaps on a trip. Sometimes adults reinforce this misunderstanding by talking about the person who died as having "gone on a long journey." Children who have had a family member or friend die may feel angry when the person does not call or return for important occasions.

If children do not think of a death as permanent, they have little reason to begin to mourn. Mourning is a painful process that requires people to adjust their ties to the person who has died. An essential first step in this process is understanding and, at some level, accepting that the loss is permanent.

Concept 2: All Life Functions End Completely at the Time of Death

Very young children view all things as living—their sister, a toy, the mean rock that just "tripped" them. In daily conversations, adults may add to this confusion by talking about the child's doll being hungry or saying they got home late because the car "died." Yet, whereas adults understand that there is a difference between pretending a doll is hungry and believing the doll is hungry, this difference may not be clear to a young child.

Young children are sometimes encouraged to talk to a family member who has died. They may be told that their loved one is "watching over them" from heaven. Sometimes children are asked to draw a picture or write a note to the person who died so that it can be placed in the coffin. These requests and comments can be confusing and even frightening to some children who do not yet understand the finality of death. In a young child's mind, if the person who has died could read a note, does it mean he or she will be aware of being in the coffin? Will the person realize he or she has been buried?

Children may know that people cannot move after they have died, but may believe this is because the coffin is too small. They may know people cannot see after death, but may believe this is because it is dark underground. These children may become preoccupied with what they perceive as the physical suffering of the deceased.

When children can correctly identify what living functions are, they can also understand that these functions end completely at the time of death. For example, only the living can think, be afraid, feel hunger, or feel pain. Only the living have a beating heart or need air to breathe.

Older Children and Adults Wonder, Too

Think about the horror films about zombies, vampires, or other characters that are dead but still retain some life functions. Many are doomed to suffer through eternity. These films are frightening to both children and adults. They are also quite popular. Why? They speak to concerns all of us have experienced about this basic concept of death.

Concept 3: Everything that Is Alive Eventually Dies

Children may believe that they and others close to them will never die. Parents often reassure children that they will always be there to take care of them. They tell them not to worry about dying themselves. This wish to shield children from death is understandable, but when a death directly affects a child, this reality can no longer be hidden. When a parent or other significant person dies, children usually fear that others close to them—perhaps everyone they care about—will also die.

Children, just like adults, struggle to make sense of a death. If they do not understand that death is an inevitable part of life, they will have misunderstandings while trying to figure out why this particular death occurred. They may assume it happened because of something bad they did or something they failed to do. They may think it happened because of bad thoughts they had. This leads to guilt. Children may also assume the person who died did or thought bad things or did not do something that should have been done. This leads to shame. These reactions make it difficult for children to adjust to a loss. Many children do not want to talk about the death because it will expose these terrible feelings of guilt and shame.

When teachers talk to children about how everyone eventually dies, children may raise concerns about the health and safety of their own family members. If individual children are particularly concerned about the well-being of their parents, teachers can ask students if they can talk with their parents. They can suggest that parents reassure their children that they are doing everything they can to stay healthy, and that they hope and expect to live a long life. For example, if a child's father died of a heart attack, the child may benefit from knowing that his or her mother has seen her doctor and had a physical exam. This shows the child that family members are taking steps to stay healthy and safe. This is different from telling children that they or their parents will never die.

Concept 4: Death Is Caused by Physical Reasons

When children experience the death of a family member or friend, they must understand why the person died. If children do not understand the real reason their family member has died, they are more likely to come up with explanations that cause guilt or shame.

The goal is to help children understand what has happened. When explaining a death to children, teachers should aim for a brief explanation that uses simple and direct language. They can watch for cues from the children and allow them to ask for further explanations. Graphic details are not necessary and should be avoided, especially if the death was violent.

Although it would be unusual for a teacher to be the first to tell an individual child of the death of a family member,[8] teachers may need to make a class announcement about someone in the school or community who has died, a classmate who has lost a parent or other family member, or another death that affects students in a classroom or school. Parents may also ask teachers for guidance about how to tell their child about death.

COMMON PROBLEMS ASSOCIATED WITH EXPLAINING DEATH TO CHILDREN

Children may not react to the news of a death in the way adults would expect. Explanations about death can confuse children in many ways. Often, misunderstandings are related to misconceptions about the Four Concepts About Death. By listening carefully to what children say and watching what they do, teachers can reinforce these essential concepts and address areas of confusion.

The following are some examples of common problems children have with understanding death:

- *Explanations and terms may not be clear.* Adults often choose words they feel are more gentle or less frightening for children. They might avoid using the words *dead* or *died,* which seem harsh at such an emotional time. However, with less-direct terms, children may not understand what the adult is saying. For example, if an adult tells a child that the family member who died is now in a state of "eternal sleep," the child may become afraid to go to sleep. Therefore, it is important to speak gently, but frankly and directly to children. Use the words *dead* and *died.*

- *Children may only understand part of the explanation.* Even when adults give clear, direct explanations, children may not fully understand. For example, some children who have been told that the body was placed in a casket worry about where the head has been placed. When discussing a death, it is a good idea to check back with children to see what they understand. You might say, "Let me see if I've explained this well. Please tell me what you understand has happened."

- *Religious concepts may be confusing.* It is appropriate for a family to share its religious beliefs with children when a death has occurred; however, religious beliefs are often abstract and difficult for young children to understand. It is helpful to provide the facts about what happens to the physical body while supporting the religious beliefs held by the family. Ideally, the family will tell the children that the person has died and clarify that the person no longer thinks, feels, or sees. They might then explain that the person's entire body was placed in a casket and buried, or that the body, which cannot feel anything, was cremated. In some faiths, the family might add that there is a special part of the person that cannot be seen or touched, which some people call the spirit or soul. They can explain that this part continues on in a place we cannot see or visit, which is called heaven.

When students are confused about religious beliefs and the physical state of a dead person's body, teachers can focus on the second concept, which is that all life functions end completely at the time of death. In public schools or secular private schools, religious discussions are a matter for families and not part of the classroom instruction. However, families might appreciate guidance on how to help their children understand what may appear to be conflicts between religious beliefs and the physical reality of death. These explanations can help children come to a better understanding of both.

When children are learning about death or personally experiencing bereavement, they may mention a belief in heaven. These beliefs can be comforting to children, and it is important to give children opportunities to express them. Teachers can then affirm that people have different religious beliefs, and that all beliefs are respected in the school setting.

Teachers who acquire a clear understanding of the Four Concepts About Death have some of the most effective tools available for supporting students, especially young students, and for responding to their questions or misunderstandings about death.

HOW MUCH CAN VERY YOUNG CHILDREN UNDERSTAND?

Even infants and very young children respond to the death of those close to them.[9] They miss the familiar person's presence. They are sensitive to the emotions being expressed around them, and if surviving parents are distressed, infants and toddlers notice. They may have trouble eating and sleeping. They may even lose weight.

Parents and preschool teachers often wonder how much very young children can understand about death. When a death occurs, it is difficult to know what explanations will be most useful to them. There are, however, a number of ways very young children can understand aspects of death, such as the absence of a loved one, and the permanence of loss.

Sometime in the second half of the first year of life, children in cultures all over the world begin to play the first of many games that help them understand the concepts of death. It is known as Peekaboo. In this game, infants fix their attention on someone and then experience a brief separation. This is followed by heightened awareness and concern, then by joy at the reunion. This is a game of loss that infants and toddlers will play over and over again as they attempt to understand and cope with loss, even if it is temporary. Peekaboo translates literally from Old English as "alive or dead."

As they grow older, young children will play Hide and Seek and other similar games. As the games become more sophisticated, so do children's understanding of temporary and permanent loss. When explaining death to children, simple terms they have learned and used in games and stories, such as *all gone*, will help. They may not understand all of the concepts fully at first, but providing them with the language to talk about these ideas helps them develop the concepts when they are ready and able.

It is important to explain the death of a close family member to young children. They may need to hear the concepts many times before they fully understand them, but in time they will grasp the concepts and, similar to older children, they will strive to make meaning from their experiences and cope with their sense of loss.

All Gone

Eva sensed something was happening. She was 20 months old, and she and her family had just driven to her grandparents' house. This was usually a happy occasion, but this time everyone was very sad. "Happen, happen?" she asked. Eva's father said her grandmother had just died.

Her grandmother had been ill as long as Eva had known her, but she did not understand what *dead* meant. Grandma always smiled when she saw her, gave her cookies and other treats, and laughed when Eva sat on her lap. Eva went looking for her grandmother in her room but found it empty. She came back out. "Grandma?" she asked. Then her father said again, "Grandma died."

"Grandma died?" Eva asked, confused by a word she did not understand.

"Grandma is all gone," her father explained.

"All gone?" Eva asked. She ran to get one of her books and brought it back, turning to the page where the baby had turned over her cereal bowl. "All gone!" she exclaimed. Then she turned to her father and asked, "Grandma all gone?"

"Yes," her father said.

Eva ran to her grandfather and grabbed him around the knees. "Grandpa all gone?" she asked.

"No," her grandfather answered. "Grandpa is fine."

From that point on, Eva never went looking for her grandmother again. She demonstrated that she understood many of the concepts about death, such as irreversibility—her grandmother would not return—and inevitability—one day her grandfather would die as well.

HOW MUCH DO ADOLESCENTS UNDERSTAND ABOUT DEATH?

Adolescents begin to develop increasingly complex abilities to analyze and understand abstractions. It makes sense that abstractions about death would be easier for teens to master than younger children, and, in general, this is true. However, teens who have experienced the death of a friend or family member often find themselves struggling, just as adults do, to accept the Four Concepts About Death as they relate to a personal loss. Teens say a number of things that illustrate this. The following are some examples:

- "I keep imagining I see my brother in a crowd or hear his voice in the next room—I just can't believe I will never see him again."
- "Somehow I still feel like my mother can hear or see me."
- "While I know that anyone can die, I just never realized that could include my own father."
- "I just don't understand why he died and wonder, deep down, if it was because I made him so sad."

As with younger children, teens will benefit from authentic and caring inter-est and a chance to respond to open-ended questions, which can often reveal questions, concerns, and even a persistent misunderstanding about the meaning of death. Chapters 4 and 5 offer guidelines for talking to children, including adolescents, about death.

HELPING ALL CHILDREN LEARN ABOUT DEATH

Teachers who take classroom time to address concepts about death, grief, strong emotions, and supporting friends who are grieving are giving all children tools they can use during challenging times in their lives. This sort of preparedness is especially helpful when children do experience a death. They will already under-stand the basic concepts about death, which helps minimize some of the confusion. They will also understand that their feelings will probably be power-ful, that they may feel guilty or have other confusing feelings, that their feelings will change over time, and that they can receive support from friends and family.

The following are some important points for teachers to remember as they think about offering such lessons:

- *Small efforts have important effects.* Students have an amazing range of life experiences. Teachers cannot possibly know about all of them, and many will never hear about some of the most powerful events in their students' lives. Yet, virtually every class will have at least one student, and often several, who have experienced the death of a family member or close friend. Simple lessons and concepts about death and grieving can help children master challenges in ways teachers do not expect or realize.

An Important Message

David Schonfeld, coauthor of this volume, was invited by a teacher to speak to her class of third and fourth graders. There were 20 children in the class. During their discussions he learned that more than half of the students had experi-enced the death of someone close.

David spoke with them for about 45 minutes, covering much of the general information in this book. He talked about some of the things people feel and think after someone they know dies. He said that most people find it helpful to talk about their feelings and about the person who died. He men-tioned that people often feel guilty when someone they love dies and wonder if they could have done something to prevent the death. The class discussed ways to support friends who had experienced a loss and how to receive support themselves if needed.

It was a straightforward presentation, and the children were interested, participated actively, and seemed to benefit from the discussion. Although many had been through difficult experiences, nothing disturbing or troubling occurred during the class.

About a week later, David received a collection of brightly illustrated, hand-written thank-you notes from the class. One of them said, "Dear Dr. Schonfeld,

Thank you for talking to our class. Now I realize it was not my fault my dad killed himself. Have a happy Valentine's Day. Love, Natalie."

This is a moving example of the way matter-of-fact discussions about death and other challenging topics help children in ways we might not anticipate. Although Natalie certainly has many issues that remain regarding her father's suicide, the discussion seemed to make it easier for her to communicate her feelings of guilt. It is likely she will find other opportunities to share this with caring adults in her life. Talking about her feelings is an important step toward adjusting to this tragedy. Often, very simple comments and interventions have profound effects on children who are struggling with some aspect of grief.

- *Simple strategies keep discussions positive and productive.* Some teachers worry that discussions about death and grief will become negative or upsetting to children. Although it is possible that children may become upset, it is always important to remember that it is the feelings of grief and loss—and the death itself—that are upsetting. Teachers can watch for signs of distress among students. It is appropriate to check with a student who is upset (e.g., see the story "Classmates Offer Support" later in this chapter). Students should always be invited to talk with a teacher after class if they have additional questions or concerns.

    In general, these conversations help children recognize and identify their feelings, express them appropriately, and think about ways to receive support when they need it. They give children a better sense of the range of feelings people may have in response to a death, and usually reassure them that their own feelings and experiences are normal.

How Do You Feel Better?

A fifth-grade student died suddenly and unexpectedly. The teacher in the third-grade class shared this information with his students. He talked with them about what it meant when someone died. His students then began to share their stories of loss and sadness. Many of these were unrelated to the death of their schoolmate. As the discussion went on, some of the children became tearful and seemed to be becoming more upset. The teacher then asked the class if anyone could share an example of something they did or something that someone did for them that helped them feel better when they were sad. His students eagerly began to share examples of support and coping. One student played with his dog. Another student's mother talked with her and helped her understand and cope with difficult feelings. One girl liked to ride bikes with her friend next door. A boy's brother took him to a basketball game and told him he was there for him and that they could talk any time. A girl's father cuddled with her as they read a book. The tone of the classroom discussion became more positive and uplifting as the children focused on ways to deal with distress; however, the conversation did not in any way diminish their expressions of sadness or shift attention away from their own experiences and needs.

- *Lessons about death and grief prepare children to support their peers.* Discussions about death, grief, and sadness give children greater skills in expressing their own feelings and having their needs met. As a result, they will have fewer fears and worries and be less likely to engage in hurtful teasing about death or grief. They will also demonstrate greater empathy for peers.

Classmates Offer Support

A second-grade class was watching a short educational video about death and grief. The narrator made the statement, "You might remember an event such as the death of a pet. This could make you sad." One of the students began crying. The teacher, seeing the boy crying, stopped the video. The other students looked up at her and said, "Hey! Why did you stop the movie?"

The teacher pointed out that the movie seemed to be upsetting one of their classmates. They all turned to the student who was crying. One boy in the class got up from his desk, walked over to the counter, and got some tissues for the crying student. Another went over to the student's desk and put his arm around him.

"What should we do now?" the teacher asked.

The student who had gone to comfort the crying boy said, "It's up to him. If he wants to keep watching, we'll keep watching. If it makes him too sad, we'll do something else." The other students all nodded their heads in agreement.

The crying boy took a big breath and sighed. He seemed calmer. He thought for a moment, and his friends continued to reassure him. "Let's watch the movie," he said.

The students returned to their seats, the movie went forward, and the class had a good discussion about the material afterward.

When the class was over, the teacher spoke alone to the boy who had been upset. "What was going on for you when you started crying?" she asked.

"Oh, I just felt very sad about my dog," the boy answered. "He died."

The teacher asked the boy if he'd like to talk to his mom or dad. Yes, he thought that would be nice. They called the mother, and the teacher briefly explained what had happened. The boy talked to her for a couple of minutes. He seemed fine by then, the mother felt comfortable with the situation, and there was no further incident.

The students in this classroom showed a level of understanding, maturity, and compassion that many people would consider unusual for 7-year-old children. What this story demonstrates is that children this age can learn these skills, given the chance, and benefit from these sorts of lessons.

HELPING CHILDREN MAKE SENSE OF THEIR WORLD

Two points are emphasized throughout this book. The first is that every student and situation is unique. No two students will feel loss or show grief the same way or respond to lessons and stories the same. Different students will benefit from different types of support. The second point is that the principles described in this book work well across a range of situations. The stories in this chapter reinforce this point. The following are some of the common themes that emerge:

- Children have deep and powerful feelings about grief and loss.

- Children are capable of considerable empathy for their peers or others who are grieving.

- Children respond well to direct, clear, and truthful communications.

- Children benefit from an understanding of the Four Concepts About Death.

- Children have good ideas about how to receive and give support and how to cope with feelings of sadness and grief. They appreciate the opportunity to share their ideas and learn from others.

- When teachers approach children in an open, nonjudgmental fashion about these issues, most are open in return and share their thoughts and feelings.

- Children look to teachers and other adults for guidance on these and other challenging issues.

ENDNOTES

1. Schonfeld (1993).
2. Speece and Brent (1984).
3. Schonfeld and Kappelman (1990).
4. Schonfeld (1993).
5. Schonfeld (1996).
6. Speece and Brent (1984).
7. Smilansky (1987).
8. For an excellent and thorough discussion of how to conduct death notification, see Leash (1994).
9. Schonfeld (1993).

3

When a Death
Occurs in a Child's Life

Teachers may wonder what to expect if one of their students experiences the death of a family member or someone else close. Although we can make many generalizations about what children typically go through, it is important to remember that children grieve in individual ways, just as adults do. The "appropriate" timeline for grief is different for every child and each unique circumstance.

COMMON REACTIONS THAT CHILDREN MAY HAVE

What we *can* be certain about is that children's reactions to a death relate to their thoughts and feelings. Sometimes these reactions make sense to teachers, parents, and other adults. At other times, they can be confusing. However, when adults understand what children are thinking and feeling, things tend to become much clearer.

The following are some common reactions children may have to death:

Children May Become Upset by
Discussions About Their Loved One

As previously mentioned, it is not the conversation causing distress, but the very painful loss felt from the death of a loved one. Talking with children provides a chance for them to show their feelings. When this is understood, it is easier to help them cope with the experience.

Children May Be Reluctant
to Talk About a Recent Death

Often children are uncomfortable talking about a death because they see that the adults around them are uncomfortable talking about it. Children may withhold their own comments or questions to avoid upsetting family members, family friends, or teachers. They may believe it is wrong to talk about such things. It is common for older children and teens to turn to peers to discuss a death. They sometimes tell adults close to them that they do not want or need to talk about it.

Children May Express
Their Feelings in Ways Other than Talking

Children may use play or creative activities, such as drawing or writing, to express their grief. Often, they come to a better understanding of grief through play and creative outlets. These expressions can offer some important clues about what children are thinking, but it is important not to jump to conclusions. For example, young children who produce very happy drawings after a traumatic death might give the impression that they are not affected by the death. In fact, this is more likely a sign that the child is not yet ready to deal with the grieving process. Similarly, teens who only want to listen to "happy" music or see "happy" movies may be signaling that they are not ready to open up to the profound emotions of grief.

Children Often Feel Guilty
After a Death Has Occurred

Young children have a limited understanding of why things happen as they do. They often use magical thinking—they believe their own thoughts, wishes, and actions can make things happen in the greater world beyond their own control. Adults may reinforce this misconception when they suggest that children make a wish for something they want to happen.

Magical thinking is useful at times. Being able to wish for things to be better in their lives and in the world can help young children feel stronger and more in control; however, there is also a downside. When something tragic happens, such as the death of a family member, children may believe it happened because of something they said, did, thought, or wished.

Older children and teens usually wonder if there is something they could have done, or should have done, to prevent the death. For example, the parent would not have had a heart attack if the child had not misbehaved and caused stress in the family. The car crash would not have happened if the child did not need to be picked up after school. The cancer would not have progressed if the child had just made sure the parent had seen a doctor.

In addition, children often feel guilty for surviving the death of a sibling. They may also feel guilty if they are having fun or not feeling very sad after a family member has died. When talking with children about the death of someone close, it is appropriate to assume that some sense of guilt is likely present. This will usually be the case even if there is no logical reason for the children to feel responsible.

Can People Tell the Future?

The mascot of the basketball team of an all-girl high school spent the night with a friend after a game. She died during the night, and her sudden death was a shock to everyone at the school. After the death, one of her friends, Kara, a senior, was speaking privately to a bereavement counselor at the school. She asked the counselor if he believed people could tell the future.

"Why do you ask?" he replied.

"This seems odd, I know," Kara answered, "but I believe I can sometimes tell the future. When I look at my classmates, I can see what college they're going to attend."

"I'm curious," the counselor said, "what this has to do with your friend's death."

"I looked at her the week prior to her death and didn't see any college, and I knew somehow that she was going to die. But I didn't tell anyone. I keep thinking I should have said something, that maybe I could have stopped it."

The counselor explained to her that after a death, people often wonder if there was something they could have done to prevent the death. They might feel guilty about something they did or didn't do that they think contributed to the death. Something that seems unimportant when it happens may feel more important after a death occurs. Because her friend's death was so unexpected, there were probably a lot of people wondering the same thing she was— whether they could have done anything to change the situation. Kara was reassured to hear that her concerns were common. She said it was helpful to know she wasn't at fault for her friend's death.

When Guilt Is More Likely

Guilt is common for children after any death. They are most likely to feel guilty when there have been challenges in the relationship with the person who died or related to the circumstances of the death. The following are some examples:

- The child was angry with the person just before the death occurred.

- The death occurred after a long illness. During this time, the child may have occasionally wished the person would die to end everyone's suffering.

- Some action of the child seems related to the death. For example, a teen was in a heated argument with his mother shortly before she died in a car crash.

Children Often Express Anger About the Death

Children may focus on someone they feel is responsible for the death. They may feel angry at God. They may feel angry at the person who died for leaving them. Family members sometimes become the focus of this anger because they are near and are "safe" targets.

Older Children and Teens May Engage in Risky Behaviors

Older children may react to a death by driving recklessly, getting into fights, drinking alcohol, smoking cigarettes, or using drugs. They may become involved in sexual activity or delinquency. Sometimes they start to have problems at school or conflicts with friends.

Children May Appear to Think Only About Themselves When Confronted with a Death

During the best of times, children are usually most concerned with the things that affect them personally. During times of stress, such as after the death of someone they care about, they may appear even more self-centered. Yet, after a tragedy, we often expect children to rise to the occasion and act more grown-up. It is true that children who have coped with difficult events often emerge with greater maturity, but in the moment itself, most children, and even adults, may act less maturely. They may respond to the death in ways that seem cold or selfish. For example, they may respond by saying "Does this mean I can't have my birthday party this weekend?" or "Am I still going to be able to go to the college I want?" Children typically think more about themselves when they are grieving, at least at first. Once they feel their needs are being met, they will be able to think more about the needs of others.

Under Stress, Children May Behave as They Did at a Younger Age

Stress may cause some children to regress. For example, children who have recently mastered toilet training may start to have accidents. Children who have been acting with greater independence may become clingy or have difficulty with separation. Children and teens may also act less mature socially. They can become demanding, refuse to share, or pick fights with family members.

FACTORS THAT MAY AFFECT BEREAVEMENT

A number of different factors affect the way children respond to a death, in both the short and long term.[1] These include

- *Age.* Although the death will be felt deeply by all children, the specific challenges that face grieving children often change as they grow older.
- *Personality.* Some children are more resilient. Some have more difficulties with mood or social relationships. Personality factors can both help and hinder the grieving process.
- *Existing coping skills.* Some children have already developed skills for coping with powerful feelings, emotional challenges, or loss.
- *History of prior difficulties.* Students who have had previous difficulties personally or in school may have more difficulty with a loss. Students with a history of disciplinary problems, personal trauma, or loss, or those in special education programs, are at greater risk for difficulties with grief.
- *Available support systems.* When children receive strong and steady support from family, school, and community, they are likely to cope more successfully with the loss and move through the grief process in a healthy fashion. Those who have inconsistent or weak support often have more difficulty.
- *Type of death.* Children may respond differently to a death that came after a long illness, for which they were prepared, than a sudden or traumatic death.

- *Relationship with the deceased.* It is always difficult for a child to lose someone he or she loves; however, the specifics of the relationship will have an impact on bereavement. For example, the death of an absent parent who was never very involved with a child might bring up feelings of conflict and confusion. The death of a sole parent who raised the child single-handedly will evoke feelings of anxiety about who will care for the child in the future.

CHILDREN'S TIMELINES FOR GRIEF

A child's timeline for grief is a unique and personal matter. The goal of successful coping does not mean pushing or rushing children through their grief. In fact, the loss of a family member or friend is an experience that never fully leaves a person. In many ways, deep losses stay with us throughout our lives.

There are, however, some factors that can affect how much time it takes for children to move through the early phases of grief and reach a point where a return to typical functioning in school, family, and social life is possible. These include

- *How well the family functions.* Families that have a history of emotional closeness and open communication can usually offer more consistent support to grieving children. When a parent is clinically depressed or has other mental health problems, it may take a child longer to move through grief. When families are troubled by domestic violence, substance abuse, prior experiences of trauma, or the absence of a parent (e.g., working overseas, deployed in the military, in jail or prison), children often receive less support.

- *Parent coping skills.* Most parents do not have experience helping their children cope with the death of a close family member, such as a parent or sibling. Parents are usually just learning how to cope with their own feelings of grief. Those who are also able to provide effective support to their children can help them process the grief experience more successfully.

- *Provision of warmth.* Children who feel connected to and loved by their family have better emotional resources to address their grief.

- *Coping skills of children.* As mentioned previously, some children have better skills for dealing with strong emotions. These children will have greater success coping with bereavement.

- *Nature of the death itself.* Every loss of a family member or friend is difficult. Some deaths, however, are more challenging than others. Deaths by suicide, violence, or acts of terrorism,[2] for example, are difficult in ways that death by illness may not be. Children may struggle more if the family feels shame about the cause of a death, such as in the case of a drug overdose or a disease such as AIDS. Deaths that receive a good deal of media notice or community attention may also be more difficult for children.

These situations are discussed in more detail in Chapter 7.

IDENTIFYING DISTRESS IN CHILDREN

Teachers and parents often feel they can accurately assess levels of distress in grieving children. They know the children well. They are familiar with the ways they act when they are happy, sad, angry, frustrated, confused, or uncertain. They understand the children's typical expressions and behaviors.

Interestingly, close adults, such as teachers and parents, are actually more likely to *underestimate* children's reactions to death and needs for support. The following are some of the reasons:

- *Adults may not expect young children to understand death or grieve a loss.* When adults do not expect children to be grieving, they may fail to see otherwise obvious cues about their distress.

- *Children's behaviors may not communicate a sense of grief to adults.* Adults usually look for and recognize behaviors that mean grief to them—sad expressions; tears; or perhaps a quieter, more subdued way of speaking. Yet, some grieving children may be silly, impulsive, irritable, or loud. Their behavior may not communicate the distress they are feeling. They may seem "fine" to observers.

- *Children's language may not communicate a sense of grief to adults.* Many adults are used to children asking for what they want and describing what they need. When children are experiencing grief, however, they may not know how to describe what they are feeling, or they may not feel comfortable sharing those feelings with others. They may not know what kind of support would help them feel better or the words to ask for what they want.

- *Adults want children to be okay, so they tend to see them that way when possible.* When children's behaviors and language seem normal and untroubled, adults feel relieved that the children are doing well.

- *Children are sensitive to adults' feelings and often want to protect them.* Children understand that direct mention of a death can be distressing to a parent, other family members, or teachers. They often choose not to bring up topics that would make these people whom they care about uncomfortable or unhappy.

SPECIFIC CHALLENGES FOR TEACHERS

Anyone who is close to children—parents, teachers, or health care providers—might miss opportunities to support children because of the issues of identifying distress that are discussed in the previous section. Teachers, however, face some additional specific challenges in reaching grieving children. The following are some examples:

- *Children may not realize their teachers are available for discussions about death.* If children have not had personal conversations with their teachers before, starting with the topic of death is difficult. If they have a stricter sense of what's "appropriate" to discuss with teachers (e.g., asking questions about math homework or an assignment), they may feel this is not an acceptable topic. If they think of teachers as a resource for intellectual knowledge, but not the practical matters of daily living, they may not think to approach them. In addition, children may feel that their teachers are too busy or have other more important demands.

- *Children may be reluctant to start conversations about death at school.* Children often have a sense of feelings being "out of control," especially when their grief is new. They do not always know how they will respond. They may worry that if they start to share their feelings, they will become upset and have difficulty maintaining their composure in front of their peers.

- *The conversation may feel too personal.* Adolescents are especially likely to feel that revealing personal thoughts, feelings, and experiences is uncomfortable or inappropriate.

Chapter 5 discusses steps teachers can take to let students know that they *are* available to talk about such matters and how to invite them to participate in these discussions.

ATTENDING FUNERALS

Families may look to teachers for advice about whether children should participate in funerals. Families sometimes worry that a funeral will be frightening or confusing for children. However, children benefit by attending funerals, and it is helpful when teachers can support children's opportunities to attend funerals or memorial services of a family member or close friend. In fact, teachers are often the only professionals who have the opportunity to provide such advice to parents prior to the time of the funeral.

When children are not allowed to attend services, they often create fantasies that are far more frightening than what actually occurs. They are likely to wonder, "What can they possibly be doing with my mother that is so awful I'm not allowed to see?" They may also feel hurt if they are not included in this important family event. They lose an opportunity to feel the comfort of spiritual and community support provided through services.

The following are some guidelines teachers can share with families to help prepare children for services.

- *Explain what will happen.* In simple terms, it is helpful for children to know what to expect. This can include general points, such as where the service will be and who will be there. It is also useful to describe what will occur during the service, such as music, speakers, and prayers, as well as the overall tone of the event. For example, people may be crying, laughing about fond memories, or telling stories about the deceased. It is good to review some of the specific features of the service as well, such as whether there will be a casket, whether the casket will be open, whether there will be a funeral procession or graveside service, and so forth.

- *Answer questions.* Families can encourage children to ask any questions they have before the service. It is a good idea to check in with them more than once on this.

- *Let children decide whether or not to attend.* Parents can let their children know that they would like them to be there. It is often helpful to let children know that they can leave at any point or just take a break for a few minutes if they would like. If children feel quite certain they do not want to attend, it is generally best to respect this preference.

- *Find an adult to be with each child.* It is especially helpful for young children and preteens to have an adult who can stay with each child throughout the service. This person can answer questions, provide comfort, and give the child attention. Ideally, this will be someone the child knows and likes who is not as directly affected by the death, such as a babysitter or neighbor. This allows the adult to focus on the child's needs, including leaving the service if the child wishes. In some cases, teachers may offer to play this important role for a child who is or has been their student.

- *Allow options.* Younger children might want to play quietly in the back of the sanctuary during the service. This can give them a sense of having participated in the ritual in a direct way. Older children or teens may want to invite a close friend to sit with them in the family section.

- *Offer a role in the service.* It may be helpful for children to have a simple task, such as handing out memorial cards or helping to choose flowers or a favorite song for the service. Suggest something that will comfort children, but not overwhelm them.

- *Check in afterward.* It is important that family members speak to children after a service and offer comfort and love. In the days following the service, it is useful to check in again and ask the children what they thought of the service. Teachers may be able to participate in this check-in as well by speaking privately to students who have attended a service and asking how it went, what they felt, and whether they have any questions.

I Want to Be at My Parents' Funeral

A family took a short drive to attend a family get-together. On the way, they were involved in a crash. Both parents were killed. The 8-year-old daughter, Hana, was seriously injured with many broken bones and internal injuries. She was admitted to the hospital, spent time in intensive care, and was still recovering at the time of her parents' funeral 1 week later. Physically, there was no way Hana could attend the service, but she wanted very much to be a part of the ceremony and to know what happened there.

Her aunt and uncle were quite close to her, and they had told her of her parents' death. They arranged to have the funeral videorecorded. After the service, they were able to sit with their niece at the hospital and watch the service together.

Some of the staff at the hospital were concerned that watching a recording of the service would be upsetting to the girl. A few even found it macabre and wondered if showing this to Hana was truly appropriate. These concerns are understandable. Indeed, some children would not have made this request or found watching a recording helpful. For Hana, however, it was just the right thing. She felt included in the ritual of saying good-bye to her parents. She felt respected and affirmed because the family had found a way to respond to her wishes about attending the funeral. She was able to participate in the funeral in the company of her aunt and uncle, who were now to become her guardians. Their shared grief about this tragedy helped them strengthen the important bonds between them.

Wanting to Say Goodbye

The parents of a toddler were concerned when their daughter began slurring her speech and having difficulties walking. The father had ALS (amyotrophic lateral sclerosis, which is commonly known as *Lou Gehrig's disease*), and the family was already greatly burdened by the demands of the illness. They watched their 2½-year-old stumble at times and even grab her father's cane on occasion to steady herself.

The child's pediatrician referred her to a neurologist and developmental pediatrician for further evaluation. The pediatrician asked several questions. Did the child also walk without difficulty at times? Yes, she did. Did she sometimes speak clearly? Yes, most certainly. Did she ever engage in play in which she mimicked her parents by putting on her mother's scarf or her father's cap, for example, or saying a phrase exactly as one of her parents did? Yes, just like all children, she mimicked and learned from the adults around her.

The child showed no neurological problems on the physical exam. It gradually dawned on the child's parents and her health care providers that the girl had been exhibiting normal behavior by imitating her father. This episode helped her parents understand more about the ways in which she was being affected by her father's illness. They then felt more comfortable being open with her as her father's illness worsened. They made sure her preschool teachers were aware of the situation.

The father died a couple of years later when the girl was starting kindergarten. She had continued to develop a close and strong relationship with him. At his funeral, she wanted to open the casket to see him again. At first, her mother wasn't sure this would be helpful. She had heard stories about young children being traumatized by viewings of deceased loved ones. Then she thought about her own experience. She had wanted to see her husband one last time, and opening the casket just prior to the funeral had been a comfort to her. She realized that because her daughter was asking for this as well, it would most likely be helpful for her. They arranged a private time after the service to have the casket opened, and together they said goodbye to this man they loved.

The next day, the mother told the story to the girl's teacher. The teacher watched for any signs of disturbance or upset, but thought that the child was responding appropriately to her father's death. She exhibited sadness at times, talked about her father openly, and interacted regularly with other students.

CONTINUING EFFORTS TO FIND MEANING

Children's adjustment to a major loss is not completed in several months or a year. As children continue in their development and become more capable of understanding what has happened and what it means to them and their family to lose someone whom they love, they will try to find a new and more satisfying meaning for the loss. As time passes, they will face new stressors, learn new skills, and have new opportunities to cope and adjust.

For many children, the second year after a death brings new challenges that may be even more difficult than those of the first year. By this time, there is less support in place. Things have essentially returned to normal for the children's friends, neighbors, teachers, or coaches. People tend to make fewer extra efforts to check in with them. At the same time, the numbing effects of acute grief have usually worn off. In the first year after a death, children and families often experience special occasions in a sort of fog because everything is radically different. The family may not even try to make them festive or important. Yet, when they come upon birthdays, the holidays, or the start of a new school year for the second time without the family member who died, it is clear that these important family events will *never* be the same. The intensity of these second-year experiences can be quite a blow to children who were expecting to start feeling better.

Sometimes children experience difficulties or raise concerns years after a death. For example, a 2-year-old might adjust reasonably well after the death of her mother, but then have many new questions and concerns at age 7. Now that she understands what a heart attack is, she may worry that she will have similar medical problems or begin to become very concerned about her father's high blood pressure. She may also start to ask questions about the circumstances of her mother's illness or death (e.g., Did she exercise regularly before she died? Had she ever been told that she had heart disease?).

An adolescent might have a challenging first year after the death of a family member and then have a couple of years where things seem back on track. Suddenly, while making the transition to college, a great deal of anxiety and uncertainty emerges.

These are examples of the ways an important loss stays with us throughout a lifetime. A boy who lost a father at a young age will probably ask himself as a pre-teen and adolescent, "What kind of guidance would my dad be giving me if he were still alive?" As he moves on to a career or college, he might ask, "What sort of work would my father think was good for me?" If he marries and has children, he will wonder, "What advice could my dad have given me about being a father?" When his own children are the age he was at the time of his father's death, he might worry acutely about his own mortality. Sad feelings from that time in his life may resurface. He will continue to miss the modeling his father might have given him about being the parent of an adolescent, the parent of a young adult, and a grandparent.

Teachers who understand this ongoing quality of grief in children are better prepared to recognize the presence of grief responses in students who have experienced the death of a family member or friend in the past. Ongoing sensitivity and support for these experiences can be extremely helpful for children. This topic is discussed further in Chapter 8.

CUMULATIVE LOSS

Some communities experience extremely high rates of ongoing violence. In neighborhoods where there is significant gang-related activity, the deaths of teens, young children, and others may be so common that individual children there have experienced many losses. This is described as *cumulative loss*.

Teachers in these communities may have the impression that their students do not want to talk about death or the impact of these losses. "This happens all the time here," one teacher remarked after several students were shot on their way home from school one day. "They're used to it."

Even when death and violence are common, children do not get used to the situation. In fact, generally they become *more* sensitized to these issues as they continue to have these experiences. Each death may bring up the unresolved feelings of prior losses, which further adds to the sadness, stress, and anxiety. Each death or traumatic experience, therefore, is incrementally more difficult, so much so that children may feel the need to deny their feelings and reactions to avoid feeling overwhelmed. They may then appear to dismiss concerns or show no reaction.

Children want and need to talk about the important things that happen in their lives. This includes violent deaths that touch them in some way. They are looking for guidance about how to express their thoughts and feelings, how to make sense of these terrible things happening around them, and how to cope best under such challenging and frightening circumstances. It is important to give them opportunities to express themselves and to be heard by concerned and caring adults.

DIFFERENT CULTURAL VIEWS OF DEATH

Death is a vital and essential part of every culture. Beliefs, rituals, and practices about death vary from culture to culture, as well as from family to family. When a teacher and a student have cultural differences, teachers may hesitate to talk about death with the child or the family. No one wants to say something insensitive when a family is grieving. It would be virtually impossible for any single person, especially a busy teacher with many daily demands, to become completely versed in all of the ways that different cultures view death. At the National Center for School Crisis and Bereavement (NCSCB), we have worked with families from many different cultures and have found two general guidelines to work well in virtually every interaction. First, be competent and comfortable in your own culture, and, second, know that every family is unique.

Be Competent and Comfortable in Your Own Culture

The most important guideline to understanding other cultural views on death is to be genuinely competent in your own culture. A sensitive and thoughtful person who can support a child in one culture will usually find it possible to work well across cultures. The same kinds of general questions and concerns come up for children in all cultures. These include concern for self (e.g., "Will I be okay?"), concern for others (e.g., "Will my other family members and/or friends be okay?"), and questions about the meaning of death (e.g., the Four Concepts About Death).[3]

When people focus on differences across cultures, it is easy to feel uncertain about offering support to someone from a culture other than one's own. One culture may not speak the name of the dead. Another may name the next-born child after the person who died. One culture may believe each tear shed creates another hardship for the deceased, so families are quiet and restrained at funerals. Yet another culture may believe that the open expression of grief demonstrates the depth of love felt, so families weep with great emotion at the service.

Instead of trying to learn all of these features for every culture in a community, teachers can simply remember in a general way that there are different cultural traditions, practices, and beliefs. Families are usually quite grateful when a concerned teacher or other helper asks directly and sensitively for specific information about these matters. At the NCSCB, we have worked with families and professionals from cultures throughout the United States, as well as internationally in cultures as varied as those in Asia, Great Britain, Europe, Scandinavia, Latin America, and the Middle East. We often find ourselves saying, "I am not familiar enough with your culture and belief system to know how best to offer my assistance. Can you give me some suggestions about how to be helpful?" We have had great success by simply saying to people, in one way or another, "I'd like to learn about your culture. I'd like to know how to be helpful."

Every Family Is Unique

Another problem with a content-based approach to cultural differences about death is that each family interacts with these cultural elements in different ways. If you think for a moment about your own culture, you'll probably be able to identify approaches to grieving that vary from family to family. Some families adhere very closely to their culture's perspective on death, whereas others follow these precepts more loosely or not at all.

For this reason, it is also important to check in at the family level on attitudes about death. Teachers can ask an individual or the entire family for guidance. For example, a teacher can say, "Help me understand how you and your family will go through this and how I can be helpful." Cues are immediately offered, such as whether the name of the deceased is used, what the time frame for the family's rituals may be (e.g., burial within 3 days, a memorial service in 2 weeks), and whether strong religious beliefs are a part of the family's understanding. When we make assumptions about how a grieving family relates to their cultural traditions, we may miss important opportunities to offer support.

An Amish Family Remembers

When we were working with an Amish family who had experienced the death of a young child, we were surprised to see a framed photograph of the girl on the wall. Amish people do not allow photographs of themselves, especially if faces are recognizable. For them, photos are considered a sign of vanity and a form of graven image.

The grandmother told a story of seeing her granddaughter out in the yard one day, talking to a tourist with a camera. She went out to see what was happening. The girl turned to her with great excitement and said, "Look, Grandma. He has taken my picture and is going to send us a copy! I've never seen a photo of myself!" The grandmother, touched by the girl's enthusiasm, decided to allow this. Soon, the family received the photo, and the girl was pleased to see it.

Shortly after this, the girl died suddenly and tragically. The grandmother touched the photo and said, "I am glad now that we have this. It is all we have of her, you see."

This is a good example of an individual family finding its own way on a specific matter of belief, one that had particularly powerful meaning for them at the time a death occurred.

OFFERING CHILDREN SUPPORT THAT HELPS

Teachers enter their profession because they care about children. It is difficult to see children struggling to cope with a death. It can also be disconcerting to feel confused by children's reactions to death. Teachers may be uncertain about how to communicate with grieving students, an especially frustrating experience for teachers who are skillful communicators in other subjects, such as math or writing.

This is why it is so useful to understand the ways children typically understand death and know about some of the factors likely to affect grieving children. It prepares teachers to offer powerful support that can help students cope well, move forward in their lives, and continue to succeed academically. The following chapters further discuss the specific kinds of support that help grieving children.

ENDNOTES

1. Osterweis, Solomon, and Green (1984).
2. See Schonfeld (2005) for an overview of the impact of terrorism on children.
3. For an example of a cross-cultural comparison of young children's understanding of death, see Schonfeld and Smilansky (1989).

4

Support for Grieving Children

What to Do

Schools and teachers can take concrete steps that will help bereaved children. These include understanding how to be present with and express support for grieving children. Communicating clearly and effectively with children and their families is key. It is also essential to remember that grief is a painful process. There is nothing that anyone—family member, teacher, therapist—can say or do that will take away the pain or make the loss less powerful. That is not the goal of bereavement interventions.

GOALS OF INTERVENTION

What are the goals for teachers who are taking steps to give grieving children and their families support? They involve helping children in the areas that are most likely to present challenges after the death of a family member or friend. The following are six goals for teachers helping grieving children:

1. *Decrease the sense of isolation.* Grieving children may pull back from family members because they do not understand or are not sure how to respond to the grief everyone is experiencing. They may not want their own feelings to create more of a burden. They may feel guilt or shame associated with the loss. If the person who died was a family member, they may wonder what their role is in the new structure of the family.

   Grieving children also often pull back from peers because they cannot quite relate the experience of a death to their relationships with peers. They may not know what to say about the death or their grief. They may feel uncomfortable at the attention people give them or with friends' attempts to offer support. Or, they may be uncomfortable because their peers seem to be ignoring their loss. They may feel distracted or overwhelmed and less able to keep up with the usual social give-and-take of their friends. They do not want to be singled out or seen as a victim. At the same time, peers may be reluctant to reach out to their grieving friends because they are unsure what to say or how to be of support. This can be a lonely and troubling consequence of children's grief. When teachers address the topic of death in school, either as planned coursework or in response to teachable moments, they provide all children with knowledge, skills, and increased comfort so that they are more able to share their feelings and receive and offer support.

2. *Increase academic function.* Common responses to death include difficulty concentrating, easy distractibility, frustration, anger, difficulty sleeping, anxiety, and feelings of sadness. It is easy for school performance to slide under these circumstances. Support that helps children cope with their feelings also prepares them to move forward academically.

3. *Increase the likelihood children will talk with their family.* The most important source of support for grieving children is their family. Many families, however, are unsure about how to talk about a death with their children. Children may not realize these conversations are important or may not know how to get started. When children have opportunities to talk with teachers and identify their feelings, communicate their concerns, and hear words of support in response, they learn how helpful this can be and appreciate that adults are prepared to provide support. This can encourage them to seek more support from their family as well.

4. *Increase the likelihood of talk and support among peers.* Students who have participated in lessons about death and grief will understand more about the process and may be more comfortable reaching out to a peer who has experienced a loss. Students who have previously *given* support to a grieving peer may be more open to receiving similar support themselves if they experience a loss. Students who see a teacher talking with a bereaved student, even if they do not know the details of the conversation, have a role model that shows them that contact is important. When grieving students are more comfortable talking about their experiences, perhaps because they have received support to do so from a teacher, they are more likely to reach out to peers as well.

5. *Identify problems in the family.* Often children provide information that brings to light difficulties within the family. Sometimes the most helpful intervention for a child is an appropriate referral for a parent struggling with depression or anxiety.

6. *Connect with students on something of immense importance.* Students respect their teachers and emulate them when they believe their teachers genuinely care about their welfare. There are few gestures that can express caring more effectively than paying attention to a child's needs after the death of a family member or friend.

These goals may sound like a lot to aim for, but they can be achieved in fairly simple ways that do not usually require a great deal of time.

BEING WITH GRIEVING CHILDREN

As a culture, we do not often talk openly about death and the grief process, especially when children are involved. Because of this, it can be difficult to understand something as straightforward as how to *be* with children who are grieving. What does one say? How should one act? What if you have feelings of your own about this loss? What if you *don't* feel strongly about it?

The following are some suggestions for how to act and what to say to grieving children:

- *Be present and authentic.* Children are sensitive to dishonesty, and they can often tell if someone is not being truthful. Being genuine involves finding ways to show concerns and emotions that ring true for both the teacher and the children. Most teachers have emotional reactions when they hear a student has suffered the loss of a close family member or a friend. A teacher who is upset and tries not to show it will not be as effective as one who can speak directly about these feelings. A teacher might say, "I was sorry to hear about your brother's death. I feel very sad that he died. I know you must have some feelings about this, too. Would you like to talk about your brother or tell me what these last few days have been like?"

  Similarly, someone who does not have a strong emotional response should not try to manufacture one. There are effective ways to express caring and concern for children in both circumstances that leave the door open for children to recognize the support. When done properly, children can trust the genuine concern and understand that teachers are interested in hearing more from them. For example, if a teacher did not know the person who died, it would not be appropriate to say, "I will miss her, too." It would make sense to a child, however, if the teacher said, "I didn't know your friend, but I can tell she was someone who was very important to you. I feel sad that you had to experience such a loss."

- *Listen more, talk less.* It is fine to share personal feelings and express caring and concern, but it should be kept brief. Keep the focus on the children who are grieving and give them plenty of space and time to talk.

- *Avoid trying to "cheer up" students or their families.* Remember, a teacher's goal is not to take away the pain of this grief. Powerful and painful feelings will be with the survivors for some time. Comments and efforts meant to cheer people up or find something positive in the situation usually are not helpful.

- *Allow emotional expression.* Young people going through grief are often told to "be strong," "toughen up," or cover up their feelings. A more helpful intervention is to suggest they are probably having many strong feelings and invite them to talk about them. Expressing emotions is an important part of grieving. This may mean watching someone be angry, selfish, or grief struck.

- *Demonstrate empathy.* Teachers should reflect back what they see students express, directly or indirectly. It should be done with compassion and without judgment.

- *Stop harmful reactions when safety is a concern.* Some children react to grief with angry outbursts. Expressions such as these are natural and show that children are willing to experience some of the truly deep feelings that accompany profound grief. Allow grieving children to cry, shout, kick the floor, or throw down a book. If such behavior poses a risk to the grieving child or others, however, it should be stopped. Property damage is also not necessary to this process, and is not helpful to children.

When children do not have an opportunity to experience and talk about their grief, they often find it difficult to make sense of their experience and move on. Inquiries from teachers or other school staff can be immensely important in these circumstances. The following story offers a compelling example.

Can Someone Just Be Honest?

Seventeen-year-old James worked after school at a local restaurant. One afternoon, he received a call from a relative with the terrible news that his older brother had just died in an accident. His parents were on their way to meet with the police. An aunt and uncle would be by to pick up James and take him home where he could be with his younger brothers and sisters.

When the aunt and uncle arrived, they were under the impression that James did not know about his brother's death. They smiled and made small talk and acted as if nothing was out of the ordinary. Back at the family home, they gathered the children around the television to watch a movie. They chose a comedy. James could not figure out what he was supposed to do. Was he supposed to pretend he was happy? Laugh? Act as if he did not know about his brother's death? Should he tell his younger siblings what had happened? "Can someone just be honest?" he kept asking himself.

By the time his parents returned home and told all of the children about the death, a good 4 hours after he had first learned about it, James was completely confused about his feelings and responses. In the weeks and months that followed, he talked little about his brother's death. He rarely showed emotion about it. He kept on with work and school. He focused on graduating from high school and following through on his longstanding plans to join the Navy.

These were difficult times for his parents. His mother struggled with powerful grief, and for several weeks she was unable to return to work. She found it difficult to do her usual family tasks—shop for food, prepare meals, get the younger children ready for school. James stepped up and took on more of these responsibilities. Everyone was impressed with how well he was coping and the maturity he showed in helping his family.

After a few months, as his mother's acute grief started to improve, James began having more problems with his brother's death. He experienced outbursts of anger or crying. He had troubling dreams. He felt empty at times and hopeless about the future. He missed his brother more deeply, and the feelings seemed to be getting worse rather than better.

After several months, his mother brought James to talk with a bereavement counselor. At first, he could not explain why he was having these increasing problems. As he told his story, however, he realized that he had never really had a chance to experience and express the terrible grief he felt about his brother's death. He had felt a need to keep things together for himself and his family while his mother was struggling so much with her own feelings. There never seemed to be anyone for him to talk to. As she improved, his own feelings and reactions became stronger, to the point where he now felt distracted and disturbed by them.

James needed to have a place to talk about his own story—how he learned about his brother's death, how he felt about it, what this emptiness would mean in his life. His grief, however, once it emerged, was not unusual or complicated. In fact, after just a couple of meetings, he felt more settled, clearer about how he was experiencing this loss, and hopeful again about the future. He did not feel a need for further meetings. This was a simple intervention that a teacher or school counselor could have offered as well. James went on to graduate and pursue his career in the military.

What *Not* to Say

The following are some examples of well-intentioned statements that are not helpful to grieving children or their families.

- **"I know exactly what you are going through."** It is not possible to know what another individual is going through, especially in a matter as profound as the loss of a loved one. Even if you have lost family members, close friends, or a spouse, your own experience is as distinct as the children you teach.

  What to say instead:

  - "I can only imagine how difficult this must be for you."

  - "I wonder what this is like for you."

- **"You must be incredibly angry."** Anger is a natural reaction in the grief process, but it is impossible to know what someone is experiencing at any given time. Telling people what they ought to be feeling is not helpful.

  What to say instead:

  - "I wonder what kind of feelings you're having about this."

  - "Most people have strong feelings when something like this happens in their lives. Has that been true for you?"

  - "What have the last few days been like for you?"

- **"I know this must be difficult, but it's important to remember the good things in life as well."** Watching someone grieve is difficult. The desire to cheer up children or their families is understandable, but it is not helpful. What grieving families need is permission to fully experience and express their immeasurable grief or

(continued)

(continued)

anger, confusion, relief, or whatever other feelings they are having. Attempts to cheer up those who are grieving may quiet their expressions of grief, but they do not lift the powerful feelings or help them process their loss.

- **"Both of my parents died when I was your age."** Avoid statements that compete with children's experiences of loss. Children who had one parent or a sibling die may feel their loss is not as meaningful if the focus is shifted to someone who has suffered even more. Similarly, comments about another student who lost both parents last year may make children feel their situation is not as significant.

- **"You'll need to be strong now for your family. It's important to get a grip on your feelings."** The most important opportunity we can offer grieving children and their families is that of expressing their thoughts and feelings fully. Grieving children are often told they should not be expressive—that they need to grow up fast, keep it together for their family, manage their feelings, and not feel sorry for themselves. These messages tend to hold children back from experiencing the deep and powerful feelings they are having without helping them cope or adjust any more effectively.

- **"My 15-year-old dog died last week. I feel very sad, too."** It is impossible to compare losses, and generally not useful to attempt to do so. As much as possible, keep the focus on the children's experience and need for support.

What About the Stages of Grief?

Many people are familiar with the Five Stages of Grief developed about 40 years ago by Elisabeth Kübler-Ross[1] or with other models that describe the stages people move through in the grief process. These include stages such as denial, anger, bargaining, depression, and acceptance. Although these models may help us understand something about the range of experiences people have in relationship to grief, they do not by themselves accurately predict the sequence of reactions most people go through most of the time. In fact, people, including most children, experience many of these kinds of feelings at different times throughout grief. Grief is not a simple linear process. Rather than try to apply children's experiences to any specific model about grief, it is more useful to take steps to understand what an individual child is experiencing at the present time and tailor support to the child's specific needs.

COMMUNICATION: THE HEART OF THE WORK

Communication is the heart and soul of this work with bereaved children and their families. When teachers help initiate the conversations, they help children gain the skills and confidence to continue them with others.

We encourage teachers to address the topic of death and loss proactively. As described in Chapter 2, it is important to discuss death in a general way with all students before any loss is identified because it provides information and anticipatory guidance around the matter of death and grief. It is also essential for teachers to actively open communication when they know a specific student is experiencing grief. Teachers should not wait for students to approach them. A student may not realize this is an option or feel secure enough in taking the first step.

A vital power differential exists between students and teachers. This is a good thing. It helps teachers offer trusted guidance in learning and maintain order when necessary. This same difference in power makes it difficult for students to approach a teacher with questions about something as troublesome as death, however. This is not so surprising, really. Even adults are often reluctant to tell others about personal experiences of grief. They may hesitate to tell a boss or supervisor about a death, or they may minimize the challenges and distress presented by their grief. Children who observe this deference or hesitation in a parent or other family member might be even more likely to avoid troubling their teacher.

Similarly, however, a teacher's status can open up possibilities with children. Teacher authority communicates experience, wisdom, and an ability to determine what topics are appropriate to discuss. Children are often quite responsive when a teacher suggests they talk about a recent death, and they usually appreciate the opportunity to do so.

Getting Students to Talk

Students may be more likely to discuss a death with a teacher if the circumstances make the topic approachable. Teachers can help set the tone for a conversation by using the following suggestions:

- *Students feel they have permission to talk about their loss.* Children realize that the topic of a death is often uncomfortable for people. They are more likely to feel that they have permission to open these conversations if they already know a teacher is willing to discuss challenging matters. They may remember a teacher saying, "You can always ask me about anything, even if it seems like something difficult." They may know peers who have felt supported when they talked to a teacher about troublesome topics. A teacher can specifically extend an invitation to an individual child to talk about a recent death.

- *Students sense the teacher is listening genuinely.* This means the teacher is emotionally and intellectually present during the conversation and is responding directly to what the student says. Unhelpful comments should be avoided (see the box "What *Not* to Say").

- *Teachers have discussed death, grief, or other difficult topics in the past.* Teachers who have already addressed difficult topics with students have demonstrated their ability to think, listen, teach, and learn about them. Students have confidence that the teacher can handle the conversation personally and will have something useful to offer.

Steps to Invite the Conversation

This section offers some steps that teachers can take to start and sustain communication with grieving students. (More detailed examples of each of these steps are given in Chapter 5.)

- *Express concern.* Let students know directly that you have heard about the death and are thinking about them.
- *Invite the conversation.* Ask a simple, direct question, such as "How are you doing?" This invites students to engage.
- *Listen and observe.* This can take patience. Some students may need time to figure out what they want to say. Some may communicate in nonverbal ways.
- *Offer reassurance.* Feelings of grief may be strong, powerful, surprising, and unfamiliar. It is helpful for students to know that these are typical reactions. It may also be useful for them to understand that the feelings change over time and become easier to experience.
- *Continue to make contact.* Students' thoughts, insights, and feelings change over time. Many will appreciate ongoing opportunities to talk about the ways their experiences are changing.

These types of interventions give children an opportunity to find their own best way through this process. Such conversations help them make meaning of their loss while continuing to move forward in their lives.

Communication Challenges

In the same way that there are factors that increase children's likelihood of talking to teachers about grieving and death, there are also reasons why children who are grieving do not readily approach teachers about their loss. For example:

- *Students may feel overwhelmed.* They may not know where to begin. They may feel unable to manage the burden of trying to cope with their own complex feelings while protecting the feelings of others who do not necessarily want to talk about death and grief. They may worry that if they start to express their feelings, they will embarrass themselves by beginning to cry in front of their peers, or, worse yet, be unable to stop crying once they have started.

  What to do:

  - Initiate a conversation.
  - Express your concern and interest.

- Start simply with one or two open-ended questions (i.e., questions that cannot be answered with a single word, such as "yes" or "no").

- Offer to speak in private outside of class.

- *Students may lack a clear sense of what support would be helpful.* Students may not fully understand what has happened or the implications that the death has for their life. They may not have personal models for seeking support. They may not realize that talking to someone, such as a teacher, would be helpful. In addition, they may not think they have anything to say.

What to do:

- Ask open-ended questions.

- Include some questions that guide students toward useful answers. For example, ask students how they are doing, how their family is doing, what kinds of support they are finding, and so forth.

- *Students may not want to stand out from their peers.* When everything else in their life feels like it is in turmoil, they may want to feel like they are just a regular student, doing regular things. They may be embarrassed at the idea of receiving any sort of special attention.

What to do:

- Offer a private conversation.

- Seek out a one-to-one conversation in a typical setting, such as the playground, a common area, or the classroom during a conference about a homework assignment that every student is having.

- Acknowledge the concern directly. For example, make a statement such as "I've sometimes talked to students going through a loss who wish everyone would just treat them normally instead of making a big deal about it. I wonder if you're feeling like that."

- *Students may feel more comfortable turning to peers.* Students may not think of teachers as a resource for this kind of support. This is especially true of adolescents.

What to do:

- Acknowledge the importance of receiving support and ask students who they are able to talk to.

- Ask if there is an adult in their lives whom they can talk to about these things.

- Offer to be available if students wish to talk at some future time.

They Acted Like Nothing Had Happened

Teresa was a 16-year-old high school junior when her mother died. She came from a close family and was able to get helpful support from her father, siblings, cousins, aunts, and uncles. She had several good friends who came to see her in the period immediately after the death, and most spent the day of the funeral with her. Everyone talked about the ways they had loved or respected her mother, the ways they missed her, and how they would keep her memory alive in the future.

She returned to school a week after the funeral. She felt ready to bring her attention back to her studies, but she also knew that everything was going to feel different to her now. She wondered what her teachers would say and how she might respond. Would one of the school counselors contact her? Would she cry? If she did, would she feel okay about it?

Her teachers didn't say anything. No counselor contacted her. No coach or club sponsor spoke up. Former teachers did not approach her. "It was so strange," she said later. "The school acted like nothing happened, like nothing was different. But for me, *everything* was different."

Teresa didn't have a specific idea about what she expected or wanted. "I just knew they should have done something. It wouldn't have even mattered that much to me what it was—just someone acknowledging that I'd gone through this incredible experience that had completely changed my life."

She was lucky to have strong support among her family and friends. Her transition back to school would have been easier for her if even one or two teachers had spoken to her directly about her mother's death.

Talking About Religious and Spiritual Issues

Public school teachers and those working in nonparochial private schools are usually wary about any discussions that might touch on religious or spiritual issues. Many teachers wonder if discussions about death and grief will cross the line and set the teacher up for parental complaints or other problems.

It is important to remember that the Four Concepts About Death are a set of facts and principles that do not conflict with religious and cultural beliefs. At the National Center for School Crisis and Bereavement (NCSCB), we have used these concepts extensively in many different religious and cultural settings and have never experienced any meaningful disagreement about them. We know of no religion that has a conflict with these concepts.

We suggest that teachers' interventions focus on clarifying the Four Concepts About Death and allowing children opportunities to describe their thoughts, feelings, and other experiences. These conversations are unlikely to create conflicts about religious beliefs with families of any faith or of none.

Religious concepts themselves are usually quite abstract. We agree that outside of parochial schools, teachers will not be teaching these abstractions. If students do ask questions specific to religious tenets, teachers can acknowledge that different families have different religious beliefs. For example, if a child asks what heaven is like, it is appropriate to acknowledge that different families have different beliefs about heaven. Teachers can suggest that they talk to their parents for more help understanding this issue.

In the work of the NCSCB, we have never experienced complaints about religious matters from parents. We think it is prudent, however, for teachers to have a set statement that can be used in response to questions about religious beliefs in discussions with any students, including those who are experiencing grief. Teachers may choose a response such as, "Your question touches on religious beliefs, and there are many different opinions about this matter. In our school, we respect different religious beliefs, but we do not teach about religion. This is why I am going to ask you to talk to your parents about this. I think they can help you answer this question."

If a parent does complain about a conversation, the teacher can easily repeat back the standard statement and clarify that no inappropriate teaching occurred. In addition, when a teacher uses this statement consistently in such instances, other students can affirm that this is the typical protocol. This can help everyone be clear about any conversation that took place and keep their focus on the needs of the grieving student.

It is also useful to recognize that these more abstract questions are often rhetorical in nature for older children. When grieving children say, "Why would God let something like this happen?" they may simply be asking the same question adults ask at times such as these. They are not asking, "What is my religious belief?" Rather, they are saying, "How can I possibly make sense of this complex world?" This topic is discussed further in Chapter 5.

The Vodun Religion and Zombies

An NCSCB staff member was speaking about how broadly accepted the Four Concepts About Death are across various religions. He qualified this by stating that the Vodun religion, or voodoo, may be an exception. This West African religion is said to have roots that go back thousands of years. African slaves brought some of the practices and beliefs to Haiti and the West Indies. Zombies—those who experience a sort of "living death"—are a genuine part of the Vodun religion.

A member of the audience who had studied Vodun while living in Africa clarified that the religion was *not* an exception. The general image of zombies as dead people who were resurrected by others who had control over them was based on the myths of Hollywood movies and popular fiction. In fact, he explained, there *are* zombies in Vodun, but they are living people who are under the influence of drugs administered by sorcerers or others intent on controlling their actions. He was eager to correct misperceptions about these religious beliefs.

At the NCSCB, we continue to find that the Four Concepts About Death are widely accepted across different religions and cultures. It is possible that there are belief systems that are in disagreement with some of these points, but we have not encountered them in our extensive work here in the United States or internationally.

HOW MUCH TIME DOES THIS TAKE?

One obstacle we find when we talk to teachers about matters of death and grieving is their concern about how much time the suggested actions will take. Some teachers wonder if they are adequately prepared to do this kind of work. They worry that they may make things worse for children or their families.

"This is too much work," some teachers have told us. "We don't know how to do this kind of complicated intervention. This is social work, not teaching."

Through the NCSCB, we have worked with thousands of schools around the country and throughout the world. We have consistently found that, most often, these interventions take a relatively short amount of time. With a little training and understanding, as is found in this book, teachers can effectively help grieving children. They can use the same skills they are already using to teach and listen to children and to communicate with families. Most teachers find it fairly easy to address the necessary matters related to grief and death, particularly when they are supported by their colleagues, schools, and districts. (Chapter 12 discusses how teachers can receive support for themselves and their colleagues.) The benefits of teacher intervention can be significant. In fact, the positive outcomes ultimately *save* time because they help prevent problems such as acting out, poor academic performance, absenteeism, or other concerns.

There will be times, however, when children's problems will take up time that teachers do not feel they have. The following are some guidelines that can help minimize this problem:

- *Recognize that most people appreciate when teachers show concern.* Grieving students and their families may feel confused or uncertain about what the children need and how schools and families, working together, can help. They appreciate learning that there are steps that help make the grieving process easier for children.

- *Most families will take advantage of help that is offered.* When families feel that they are being listened to and have a sense that genuine needs are being addressed, they tend to become more engaged and more likely to accept assistance and follow recommendations. Sometimes being very specific is helpful. For example, teachers can say, "Can we meet tomorrow at 4:00 to talk about some of these issues?"

- *A clear focus on death and grieving can sometimes make interactions with families more efficient.* In one instance, a mother was intent on discussing her son's problems with homework. He was not completing his assignments on time, the quality of his work was poor, and he did not respond well to her reminders to do his work. She asked the teacher for guidance about managing her son's study habits because she felt that she could not control his studying. She contacted the teacher repeatedly and complained that her son was not keeping up. She needed additional suggestions.

    The teacher set up a face-to-face meeting and asked the mother how she felt her son was doing after his father's recent death. In fact, that discussion helped the mother understand that her son's study habits were completely understandable given the circumstances. She recognized that the school was making appropriate accommodations for him, and that her most important focus at this time in their lives needed to be on her son's emotions, not his homework.

This brief and successful conversation ultimately freed up more of the teacher's time for other work.

- *Look for support from others.* Finding like-minded colleagues who can help teachers think through the conversations they might have with grieving students is helpful. Teacher in-services can be requested to address these issues. Teachers can also seek advice from a mental health provider in the school or ask if the school could invite a bereavement specialist who would be available to answer questions. When teachers feel supported in these activities, they are more likely to follow through and feel successful.

- *Set limits when necessary.* Teachers who develop effective communication skills, provide comfort and support to children, and learn to effectively express empathy may find they draw many inquiries from students. Former students may come back to talk to a teacher they loved and trusted. Most teachers want to have this kind of impact and appreciate the rewards of good connections with their students.

  There may be times, however, when teachers are unable to respond to a student's request for support. There may already be too many demands on their time or too many challenges related to grief in their own life. Teachers may have other crises in their life at the moment—relationship difficulties, a sick child, a legal problem. Their personal sense of empathy may simply be exhausted and need restoring.

  If teachers feel overwhelmed by requests for this kind of support, it is important for them to remember that they do not need to do all of it themselves. Similar to tutoring, children might choose one teacher first, but then seek support from other competent individuals if that teacher is not available. Other resources can also be used—a school counselor, school or community mental health services, a colleague, or referral to a local hospice bereavement program. Teachers should also check with a student's family to see if they are involved in a faith community where they could seek pastoral support.

- *Understand that ignoring the problem is not a solution.* It is vital that grieving children are guided to appropriate resources. Even a teacher who feels stretched too thin to offer substantive personal support can provide a useful referral. "I am so sorry you have had this death in your family," a teacher can say. "Let's figure out who you can talk to."

What is the best way to make all of this work when offering support to grieving children? The first step is simply to start the conversation by making contact with a grieving student. Once that first contact is made, straightforward strategies are usually quite successful. More specific guidelines are reviewed in Chapter 5.

ENDNOTE

1. Kübler-Ross, 1969.

5

Communication

Ways to Make Contact and Keep It Going

Even when teachers realize that it is important to make contact with grieving students, it can be difficult to decide how to approach them. Some people seem to have a natural comfort level talking about issues such as death, but many find it challenging. They are not sure how to bring it up. They worry that they will say something awkward that will cause children additional pain or discomfort.

These are natural feelings, but they can keep teachers from taking those first steps needed to open a conversation. That is why it is important to understand *how* to make contact. There are a number of ways in which teachers can make positive and helpful connections after they learn that a student has experienced a loss. This chapter discusses these techniques, which have been used successfully by teachers in a wide range of circumstances. They work in complicated situations and in situations that are more straightforward. They work with troubled or isolated students, as well as with students who have strong family and social support.

The outcomes of making contact will be different; that is, they will be as unique as every student and family. They will also depend on the teachers' relationships with the students. The benefit of reaching out in the first place, however, is almost always positive.

WAYS TO MAKE CONTACT

A number of steps can help set a positive foundation for making contact with grieving children. This section highlights four steps that are helpful for teachers.

Make the Commitment

When teachers hear that a student has experienced a loss, they should make the commitment to make contact. If teachers know the student or family well, they should consider contacting the family at home by telephone after first hearing about the death to offer condolences and support. It is important to remember that even when teachers do not know students well, expressing condolences and acknowledging the loss can be very powerful and helpful. It will also make it much easier for students to return to class when they know that their teachers are already aware and ready to provide appropriate support.

Find (or Create) the Opportunity to Talk

Usually, this is a private conversation, so it is best if teachers can find a moment when they can interact with the student one-to-one. Perhaps the student could be approached privately before or after class, in common areas of the school, or in some other setting. Teachers might also choose a regular school activity that provides one-to-one contact, such as while discussing a report or project. The student could also be asked to come in a little early or stay after other students have left for a break.

If teachers do not work directly with the student and do not have an opportunity for a one-to-one conversation, they can approach the student more generally and express concern. For example, a teacher might approach a student sitting with a couple of friends and say, "It's good to see you back at school. You and your family have been in my thoughts."

Offer Condolences and Support

A simple expression of concern and caring lets students know that their teachers are aware of their situation and thinking of them. The following are some examples of condolences and offers of support that teachers have made to students:

- "I'm sorry to hear about your father."
- "I just wanted to let you know you've been in my thoughts. I am sorry about your brother's death."
- "I'm glad to see you back here at school. I was thinking about you while you were at your mom's funeral."
- "How are you doing? I've been wondering how things have been for you since your grandmother's death."

Students' responses to these offers of condolence and support can guide teachers. The most important thing teachers are offering in this first contact is a compassionate presence, that is someone who is willing to provide support if students want or need it. It is important to listen, but it is not necessary to force a discussion. Remember, there is nothing anyone can say or do that will take away the pain or the loss. What people who are grieving usually find most helpful is someone who can listen openly to whatever they have to say.

Promote Ongoing Communication

Students who are interested in talking more may ask questions, talk about their experiences, or keep the conversation going in other ways. Teachers should continue to be guided by their comments. Students' questions should be answered in simple, age-appropriate ways. Some questions may need to be answered many times, especially (but not only) with younger children.

Teachers should offer honest answers to questions. Often, "I don't know the answer" is the best response. Teachers should also be mindful about using euphemisms and remember that it is okay, even preferable, to use the terms *dead* and *death*. Responses should be open and nonjudgmental. It is important for students to feel that they can honestly express their thoughts and feelings to their teachers. They may not have similar opportunities at home if they feel they must protect a grieving parent.

Children often do not have a sense of what they want to say or what would be helpful, so teachers should ask open-ended questions that give students an opportunity to share more about their experience if they wish. The following are some examples of open-ended questions teachers have used that keep communication going:

- "How have you been doing over the past couple of weeks?"
- "How's your Mom (sister, brother, family) doing?"
- "What's it like coming back to school?"
- "What has this past week been like for you?"
- "What sorts of things are you thinking about these days?"

As mentioned in Chapter 4, teachers may also recognize that some of the questions children ask are essentially rhetorical—they do not need a direct answer. They express a sort of philosophical dilemma about human suffering, rather than a search for concrete answers. Even elementary school-age children might ask questions, such as, "Why do people have to die?" "Why couldn't it have been somebody else's mom?" "Why do we even bother loving people if they're just going to die?"

Questions such as these often benefit from comments that give students opportunities to continue expressing frustration, confusion, and pain. The following are some examples of responses that can keep communication going if students make these kinds of comments:

- "It's really hard to understand why these things happen."
- "So many things about death don't seem to make any sense at all."
- "I can only imagine this loss leaves you with a lot of confusion and questions."
- "You're asking the questions everyone asks when someone they love dies. It's hard to make sense of it."

MAKING CONTACT WHEN GRIEF IS NOT NEW

Many children have experienced the loss of a parent or other close family member at some point in the past. With a little adaptation, these same principles for making contact also work well with these students.

For example, teachers might respond in a direct and supportive way when topics such as death or grief come up in school. These topics may arise in classroom conversations, playground interactions, or during interactions between students. Teachers who respond are letting students know they are listening, they care, and they are available for further communication if students wish.

Teachers can approach students by commenting on what they have seen or heard. Open-ended questions that express interest and curiosity often work best. The following are some examples:

- "Can you tell me more about your drawing?"
- "What were you and Maria playing during recess today?"
- "I wanted to let you know that I was surprised and moved by your essay. I hadn't realized you had a sister who died."

Teasing on the Playground

Six-year-old Justin's father died by suicide. He had cut his wrists. Justin's parents were divorced and had not been in regular contact, so Justin and his mother did not learn about the death for several months. Neither of them had been able to attend the funeral. Justin's mother felt very guilty about her ex-husband's death and barely talked about it with her son.

Justin attended school with his 7-year-old cousin, Evan, who began to tease him about the death. When Evan saw Justin, he sometimes made slashing gestures across his own wrists. He taunted Justin, saying, "Your daddy died, your daddy died" as he repeated the gestures.

When this happened at home, Justin would run to his mother crying. His mother, hearing of the taunts, would burst into tears herself. The two of them sobbed together, filled with anguish and grief. Neither seemed able to take any steps to stop the teasing.

This went on for several months. When the principal finally learned of it, she was concerned by the cruelty of the teasing. She asked for help from a pediatrician who consulted at the school. The physician met with both boys and asked them to tell him what was happening between them. Justin said, "He teases me because my daddy died."

Evan quickly responded, "Well, he teases me because I'm fat."

The physician asked Evan if he had ever experienced a loss. Yes, Evan told him, he had once had a pet die. "How did that feel?" he asked Evan.

"Sad," the boy replied.

"Is that how you want Justin to feel?"

"No!" said Evan, seeming to suddenly realize what he had been doing. "I don't mean for him to feel *that* bad. I just don't want to be teased for being fat."

Justin, a little surprised, said, "I'm sorry. I didn't mean to hurt your feelings either."

"Is there more?" asked the doctor.

The boys looked at each other. No, there wasn't anything else going on. Yes, they would both agree to stop teasing each other.

The entire intervention took about 15 minutes. After that, there were no further problems between the boys. The mother, who was depressed, was referred for mental health services and was able to improve with appropriate support.

If a teacher familiar with children's understanding of death had noticed the teasing early on, it would have been possible to resolve these behaviors much sooner. The solution was simply a willingness to talk to both students and an ability to understand what each had to say.

TALKING WITH OTHER STAFF

Another helpful strategy in maintaining productive communication with children is for the school staff to talk among themselves about their interactions with grieving children. What kinds of contacts are others having with children who are grieving? What are their impressions of children as they are coping with loss? What about children who experienced a death some time ago?

Staff members often have distinct perspectives on each student. They may have different information about the ways a child is coping. One teacher might have opportunities to see more of a student's strengths and supports. Another might see more of the challenges and frustrations. Taken together, these observations can sometimes suggest specific support that is needed and who is best suited to offer it. For example, a teacher who finds that he or she can talk with a grieving student about his interest in baseball might be the perfect person to make authentic contact about how the student is coping with his situation.

PROVIDING SUPPORT FOR SCHOOL EXPECTATIONS

Another way teachers and other school staff can keep communication with grieving students open and productive is to anticipate challenges in schoolwork and classrooms. Some students will do fine socially and academically, even after the loss of someone very close. Most, however, will have at least some of the typical responses to grief, such as difficulty concentrating, easy distractibility, awkwardness with peers, and loss of interest in schoolwork.

It is important for students to understand that these are common reactions. If they have confidence that they will receive support as they move through the process, they will feel less anxiety about their mental state and their academic performance. Teachers can take steps that help students gain this understanding. Teachers, students, and their families working together can provide support that helps students stay on track while accommodating their needs during this early period of grief.

The following are some things schools and teachers can do to help students stay on track:

- *Maintain or increase contact with the student's family.* Phone calls and e-mails are usually helpful. Family meetings can be very useful if the parent or parents are able to meet in person. These contacts can offer guidance about what grieving students often experience, address concerns of the family, and reassure students that their teacher is aware of the challenges they are facing at this time. Students and their families feel more secure when they understand strategies are in place to provide support.

- *Choose an adult or a location as a safe space.* During the first few months after a loss, children may be affected by sudden reminders of the person who died.

These are called *grief triggers* (this is explained in more detail in Chapter 8). Children may experience outbursts of anger or sadness, uncontrolled tears, feelings of emptiness, or other distracting reactions. In the middle of a class activity or focused personal work, they may find themselves thinking suddenly of their grief. For a brief period, they may feel overwhelmed or unable to concentrate or apply themselves to the task at hand. They may not wish to remain in the room to listen to a discussion of a book passage that reminds them of their mother who recently died. They may worry that they will start crying in front of their peers.

These kinds of experiences can be disconcerting to children. Talking them over with an adult who knows how to listen can help children understand more about the process of grief in general, as well as their own personal experience. They can learn skills and strategies that will help them cope with greater success over time by understanding what is happening, feeling more in control of their environment and their own responses, and knowing how to get support when they need it.

A "safe space" is a place where grieving children can take time to calm themselves if they feel troubled and to seek guidance to move through these incidents. Some possibilities for safe spaces include the counseling office, nurse's office, vice principal's office, or even an open study hall or library. In a kindergarten class, a student might be offered a special area as a safe space, such as the corner by the bookshelf or the chair next to the teacher's desk. These are places where children can temporarily escape any pressures, demands, or unpleasant interactions. Ideally, they will also be able to talk with a supportive, helpful adult as they work through the incident.

- *Establish a procedure that allows children to leave the classroom if they are feeling overwhelmed.* For some period of time after a death, it may be useful for grieving students to have permission to leave the classroom as needed. When children know they can leave if they feel overwhelmed, they will feel less anxious about returning to school after a death and will actually find it easier to remain in the classroom. Knowing they *can* leave makes them less likely to want to leave. It is similar to knowing that you can turn off a scary movie on a DVD if it becomes too frightening, which makes it more manageable than being in a theater with friends where it would be embarrassing to walk out. Most students will never need to take advantage of this opportunity, but they will appreciate the option.

  Simple communications, such as hand signals, a brief note, or a key phrase (e.g., "I need to be by myself for awhile") that do not draw attention from peers might serve as appropriate notice to a teacher. Obviously, older students can be given more independence in these matters. Younger children will need the safety of an attending adult. As schools arrange these procedures, they should apply the same safety measures they would for other situations in which students might leave a classroom.

- *Let children call a parent if they wish.* When grieving children experience sudden strong emotions, checking in with a parent or guardian can be very helpful. Children who have recently experienced a loss should have considerable freedom to make these kinds of calls.

- *Provide passes or permission for children to see the school counselor or nurse.* One of the best times to talk with grieving children is when they are *ready* to talk. If children wish to see the school counselor or nurse, teachers can help by facilitating these connections in the easiest, promptest way possible.

- *Modify assignments, tests, and school projects.* Due dates can be extended, tests postponed, or projects simplified. This is discussed in more detail in the next section.

- *Provide more frequent progress reports to students and their families.* Typical grading periods (e.g., semester, quarter, half-quarter) are really too long a span to measure progress for children in acute grief. In most cases, children will be trying to get back on track with their studies, their interests, and their social life. They may have trouble figuring out how to do this. They often focus more on areas in which they feel inadequate, and they are less aware of areas in which they are doing well.

  Frequent progress reports give teachers an opportunity to share observations about students' efforts. Teachers can ask students how they are coping, clarify anything in the lessons that is not making sense, and help students schedule additional support for learning. They can also comment positively on any contributions or special efforts students have made. These reports offer important opportunities to provide positive feedback about what students are doing well. At a time when they may wonder if their lives will ever feel "right" again, this can be reassuring.

- *Offer private time with students.* Grieving students can benefit immensely from occasional one-to-one meetings with their teachers. These might be offered on an as-needed basis, but it can be very helpful to set up a regular private meeting with bereaved students. Even 10 or 20 minutes a week gives students a chance to ask questions about coursework, express feelings about their grief experience, and benefit from the special concern of a caring teacher. Such meetings are an ideal time for teachers to ask students some of those open-ended questions about their thoughts, feelings, and experiences as they move through the grief process. It is best not to wait until academic failure becomes obvious before offering extra support. By that point, the child has to deal with grief and academic failure simultaneously, both of which alone can feel overwhelming.

Assignments and Tests

Grieving students may be out of school for some period of time—a few days or more, depending on the student and the family's circumstances. When students are in school, it is appropriate to continue giving them assignments; however, it is also proper to modify the assignments as needed. Grieving children may need help finding coursework that feels achievable or appropriate in their current circumstances. For example, if members of a fifth-grade class have been working for 4 weeks on a 10-page paper about some aspect of the state's history, a teacher could talk to a recently bereaved student about writing a more focused paper that is only 3 pages long. Or, if a high school social studies class has been doing research projects on violence prevention, and a family member of one of the students dies violently, the teacher might check to see if that student would prefer to do research on another area in social studies, such as how citizens can place an initiative on the ballot. Sometimes teachers change their plans for an entire class if one or more of the students have recently experienced a death that would be unnecessarily revisited by the planned course of study.

Testing is often one of the most difficult tasks for students who are recently bereaved. Therefore, teachers might exempt students from tests or give the tests less weight in the final grade for students who have recently experienced a loss. Teachers might also allow grieving students to take a test privately in a quiet area or allow more time to complete the work. A one-to-one meeting with a grieving student before a test or a special tutorial session might also provide support students appreciate and can use.

Changing the Course Curriculum

A serious residential fire resulted in the death of two members of a family—a child and one of the parents. Three other children in the family survived. They attended the public schools, and the oldest daughter was in high school.

These deaths had a profound effect on the community. The family was well known. The daughter was popular and had many friends at school who had known and cared about the family members who had died.

An English teacher, looking over the curriculum for the coming year, recognized that one of the books he loved teaching included a scene in which one of the leading characters died in a fire. Reading and discussing the book had always been the most dynamic lesson in the class. He could not imagine giving it up. Then he tried to imagine teaching the book—to the daughter, to her friends, to all of the students who knew this family, and to all who had simply heard about the fire. "There are hundreds of excellent books to choose from. My class will do fine without this one," he said. He changed the lesson plan.

SETTING LIMITS

Children who are grieving sometimes act in ways that challenge teachers. They are experiencing many powerful emotions. They may express anger, act selfishly, or say things that are hurtful to other students. They might break or carelessly lose things. They might speak insolently to school staff. Although a sensitive teacher can clearly see that these are expressions related to underlying grief, there may still be a need to set limits on misbehavior. There is, however, a fine line between setting limits and being punitive. Of course, teachers must take appropriate steps to keep all students safe and to promote a positive learning environment. If limits must be set with grieving students, this should be handled calmly and in a matter-of-fact way.

Sometimes, a simple, straightforward correction can help grieving children gain control of their impulses and behavior. A compassionate frame gives children a chance to see themselves in a better light, and they may strive to match that image. For example, a teacher might say, "Stuart, that was an unkind thing to say. Were you actually trying to hurt Jamal's feelings?" This gives Stuart a chance to realize he did not want to hurt Jamal's feelings and that he does not want to be mean to others.

If misbehavior is more serious, or a child does not seem to respond to this type of redirection, the teacher should meet with the student privately. This gives teachers an opportunity to make direct observations about the behaviors. For example, a teacher might say, "I know that sometimes people feel very angry when someone they love has died. I wonder if you've had any feelings like this since your father died." A more direct observation might be, "I haven't seen you behave in this way before. I wonder if the strong feelings you've been having since your father's death are playing a part in these behaviors." It is important to contact the family to let them know about these concerns. They may be unaware of their child's misbehavior or have other concerns or additional insights. It is also important to convey that the call is due to genuine concern about the child's adjustment, rather than to complain about the child's behavior.

If troubling behaviors occur repeatedly, a family conference would be appropriate. A referral for supportive counseling could also be helpful. These issues are discussed in more depth in Chapter 7.

KEEP MAKING CONTACT

The death of a family member or friend is a fairly common event in the lives of young people. Although the questions grieving children have are sometimes complex, most often they are straightforward and direct. Sometimes they want to understand facts about death. Sometimes they need help understanding how to explain themselves to friends. Sometimes they simply need to know that a trusted, caring adult believes in them and believes that they will get through this confusing experience. They also need to know that an adult is there to provide support over time as they struggle to adjust to the loss.

I Don't Want to Say My Dad Is Dead

Sofia's father died near the end of first grade. Sofia's second-grade teacher was aware of the death and made an effort to notice how her student was coping. Sofia was doing well in school. She was close with her mother, and she received strong support from her family. Her first-grade teacher described her as bright and talkative. She said that Sofia was always one of the first children to reach out to meet new people and get to know them. In second grade, however, she seemed more reserved with her new classmates, and she seemed uncomfortable interacting socially with several girls who were new to the school.

The previous year she had talked openly about her father shortly after he died, but her second-grade teacher never heard her talking about her father.

Worried that she might be depressed, the teacher arranged for Sofia to see a counselor. The counselor asked her how she was feeling after her father's death, and Sofia readily acknowledged that she was having a problem.

She explained, "My classmates ask me what my dad does for a living. I don't want to say he's dead—it makes me feel sad."

Sofia and the counselor explored several different possibilities about what she could say. Perhaps she could say he had gone on a long trip? No, that wasn't true, and she didn't want to be dishonest. Could she say she didn't want to talk about it? No, that didn't seem friendly. People would think she was stuck up.

Then the counselor asked, "Could you say, 'My father is no longer alive?'"

Sofia thought about this, and then she tried it out. "My father is no longer alive." When she said this, she didn't feel sad.

"Yes," she said. "I can say that. This solves my problem!"

Prepared with this phrase that said just what she wanted, she returned to her class, began socializing more freely with her peers, and sometimes talked about her father with her new friends.

We encourage teachers to use these "making contact" strategies on a regular basis with students, not just in instances of death, but on other matters that may appear sensitive or difficult. The more that teachers can express to students that they are listening, they care, and they are available to talk, the more students will be able to come to them with their questions and concerns, whatever the topic may be.

6

Working with Families

Working with families is something most teachers do regularly. They talk with parents at back-to-school nights, open houses, field trips, school meetings, and parent conferences. They communicate through e-mails, memos, phone calls, report cards, class web sites, and newsletters. These ongoing communications help families take steps to support their children's learning and participation at school.

Contact with families is especially important for children who are grieving. As mentioned in previous chapters, challenges with concentration and learning are common for grieving students. Most will have some level of school problems for a period of time after a family member or friend dies. Talking with family members helps teachers understand more about what the children and their families are experiencing, lets children know that their families and teachers together are concerned, and helps everyone have more realistic expectations and understanding about what will happen in the coming months.

TEACHERS' AND SCHOOLS' SPECIAL ROLE WITH FAMILIES

Chapter 1 reviewed some of the reasons teachers and schools can play a special role in helping children learn about death and helping grieving children cope. For some of the same reasons, teachers can play a unique and important role for families experiencing bereavement. The following are some examples:

- *Schools are familiar and teachers are trusted.* Schools are part of children's everyday lives. The staff and setting are familiar to families. Teachers are respected for their expertise and knowledge. All of these qualities make information from teachers valuable to many families.

- *Families are often looking for guidance.* Grieving families are usually challenged by their situation and often have questions about how to help their children. Many families do not seek advice from health care providers, mental health specialists, or pastoral services, but they will have contact with their children's teachers. Even when they have received advice from other professionals, they often have additional questions about what to do for their children and family. Sometimes families are skeptical of advice provided in a counseling or mental health context. The same information coming from a teacher, however, may seem less clinical and more "normal." They may be able to accept this guidance more easily.

- *Teachers have special knowledge that other providers do not have.* Teachers spend considerably more time with children than most health, mental health, or pastoral providers ever will. They see aspects of children's behavior and performance that may not come up around the doctor, counselor, or even a parent. They have a particular understanding of how grieving children are coping with the process of learning, which is less likely to come up in other settings.

- *Children may behave differently at school.* Children may experience and express frustration or sadness at school, but they may cover up those feelings at home. They may feel a need to protect their parents from seeing their grief. They may be taking steps to avoid "rocking the boat," without even realizing that they are hiding their feelings. School is sometimes the setting where children are able to express powerful feelings that they are not revealing elsewhere.

- *Teachers are in an excellent position to make referrals that can help families.* Most families may be unaware of bereavement support services within the community, or they may feel that their grief is something they should be able to handle on their own. However, families may accept referrals from teachers that they would not as readily accept from other sources.

They Have No One Else to Talk to

One of the authors of this volume, David Schonfeld, served for several years as a consultant to an elementary school in a major city. The school had 800 children in grades prekindergarten to second grade.

One Monday morning, David arrived at the school and was immediately greeted by the principal. "We have had a tragic event in our community," she told him. She reported that one of the students was visiting his grandfather's apartment over the weekend with some other children. At one point, the man excused himself, went into the bathroom, and shot himself in the head. The children were alone when they found his body. The principal asked David if he would meet with the student and begin to help him make sense of this tragedy, as well as guide the student and his family to additional services.

The principal then explained that she had another request. She asked if David would also be willing to meet with several older children who were at the apartment at the time and who were former students of the school. A baby sitter who had been helping to care for the children that weekend had also been present. Knowing his answer ahead of time, she had already arranged for all of these children to be at the school; they were waiting to meet with him. The principal reassured David that she had spoken with the parents of all of the children over the weekend: "They don't know who else to speak to. They need your help right now. It's not like we can just send them to the other schools before we help them deal with what they heard and saw. Their parents sent them here because they knew we would help them."

Thanks to this principal, who was a tireless and effective advocate for her students, their families, and the community, these children were able to begin talking about the experience. They were connected with ongoing services. Their parents, who had turned first to the principal, received the services that their children and families desperately needed to deal with this tragedy. This was clearly a sign of the enormous impact this principal had within her community and in the lives of her students.

OFFERING GUIDANCE TO FAMILIES

In offering guidance to grieving families, teachers can support the use of open, clear communication about death and grief. When children receive support from their parents and other family members, it helps the entire family cope. The family sees that it can stay close even though the feelings of grief might be very strong.

When teachers talk with parents, many of the same guidelines for talking to grieving children are helpful. After all, most of the communication strategies described in Chapter 4 work with people of all ages who are coping with a loss. They include such things as being present and authentic, being willing to listen, avoiding trying to cheer people up, and allowing people to express their feelings.

Similar to talking with children, it is important to stay open-minded and nonjudgmental about the emotions parents might express. In periods of acute grief, many of our "filters" are down. People often say things bluntly or reveal things that they might not say in other circumstances. Parents may describe frustration with their children, bitterness about the person who died, old family secrets, or other troubles. Teachers who set a stage that welcomes these expressions gain important information about their students' home environments and may be able to make better judgments about what will be most helpful for students and their families.

The following are some of the issues that teachers can discuss with parents:

- *A parent's role is essential.* Let parents know that their children are looking to them for help in understanding these confusing and troubling events. More than anyone else in their lives, children look to parents for guidance about how to cope.

- *Children are concerned about their parents.* Children wonder how their parents are coping. They worry about their parents' health and survival. If someone close to them has just died, does this mean that others they love and count on could die too? It is important for parents to find ways to offer honest reassurance to their children.

- *Children are also concerned about themselves.* Particularly after the death of a parent, children may worry that everyone else will die and leave them all alone. Who will take care of them, give them shelter and food, and keep them safe? In these situations, children may benefit from knowing that there will always be someone who knows and cares for them. Sometimes it helps to explain that parents make plans for their children just in case of the highly unlikely possibility that both parents would die while their children are still young.

- *Children need support to understand death.* It is helpful for parents to under-stand the Four Concepts About Death (discussed in Chapter 2), why they are important for children, and how to explain them to children. Teachers can review these concepts with parents of young children and offer suggestions about how to discuss them with their children.

- *Direct, clear language is important.* Many of us have been taught to use euphe-misms about death. As explained in Chapter 2, it is important to speak gently but frankly with children and to use direct words, such as *death* and *died.*

- *Honesty is essential.* Children must understand the truth about the death of a loved one. The best possible place for them to hear that truth is from within the family. Some deaths are disturbing, such as homicides, suicides, and random acts of violence. Understandably, parents hesitate to share the details of these kinds of deaths with children, especially if they are young. As difficult as it may be, honesty is essential. If the family does not tell children the truth about what has happened, the children will learn the facts at another time. Usually, this will happen much sooner than a family imagines, and often the circumstances are not ideal. Children may be taunted by a classmate, come across a news report about the death, or overhear a comment by a neighbor. These experiences can be deeply troubling to children, and they often make it difficult for them to trust their family regarding important issues in the future.

   Teachers may be able to suggest ways to talk about a troubling death to children. As mentioned in Chapter 2, graphic details are not necessary and should be avoided. These are situations in which a bereavement counselor or mental health professional may also be able to help parents find ways to explain the death and help the children cope.

   Teachers may also be able to suggest additional resources that can help support families coping with grief. For example, there may be a bereavement or hospice program in the community that offers support groups for children and families. Special programs may also be available for grieving children, such as camp experiences. In addition, there are web sites and written materials that can also be helpful.[1] (See the Resources section of this book for more information.)

It's So Hard to Tell My Son

Nate was 5 years old when his father became ill. His father was diagnosed with depression and hospitalized after a suicide attempt, but his parents chose not to tell the boy about this. Instead, his mother simply told Nate his dad was away on business.

After being released from the hospital, the father was enrolled in treat-ment and prescribed medications for his depression. His condition worsened, and he was hospitalized a second time after a serious overdose. This time, Nate's mother told him his father had to go to the hospital because he was vomiting, but he would be home again soon.

When Nate's father was discharged from the second hospitalization, he returned home. Moments later, he left to go to his office. Once there, he took the stairs to the roof of the building and jumped to his death.

Nate's mother was devastated and felt guilty that she had not supervised her husband more carefully when he returned home. She could not bear the thought of explaining to her young son the truth about how his father had died. Instead, she told Nate, "Daddy fell and bumped his head, and he died."

Nate became increasingly anxious after his father's death. He began to have frightening dreams, often about hitting his head. He was having problems getting along with peers at school. He and his mother were referred for counseling.

Nate's mother arrived to her first counseling visit exhausted. Nate had been up much of the night after having another nightmare about hitting his head and dying. She told the counselor about her reluctance to tell Nate about his father's suicide. "I just don't think he is ready to know. I *will* tell him when he's older—just not yet."

The counselor looked at her. "The explanation you've given him doesn't seem to have been very satisfying for Nate," he observed.

She agreed that it didn't seem to be working. The counselor spoke to her gently. "You may want to reconsider this," he told her. "From my experience, I've seen that children do best when they have an honest, appropriate explanation of what happened."

He went on to point out that it was only a matter of time before someone else told Nate the truth about his father's death. "It is very difficult information to share, I know. But it will be best if it can come from you."

The mother reluctantly agreed, and she and the counselor spent the rest of the session working out how she could tell her son the truth of his father's death. She was able to follow through on this plan. Although Nate continued to miss his father very much, his nightmares stopped and his behavior at school became more appropriate.

INFORMATION ABOUT THEIR CHILDREN

Teachers can describe some of the reactions children generally have to a death. As discussed in Chapter 3, children may become upset by discussions about the death, feel reluctant to talk about it, or feel guilty or ashamed about it. Letting parents know that these responses are common can help reassure parents about the reactions their children are having.

Teachers' specific observations can also be helpful for parents. For example, they can talk about how they see the student coping. This might include areas of difficulty, such as a child who has withdrawn somewhat from peers or is having difficulty concentrating in class. When possible, it is also helpful to comment on areas of strength. The child might be reaching out to friends for support or doing good work in some areas of study. The teacher can affirm that it is clear the child's attachment to the family is strong and important.

Teachers can also review what the class is studying and discuss the type of work that is forthcoming. They can describe how the student is doing academically and talk with the parent about any accommodations in lessons or tests that might be appropriate. Again, it is important to normalize these periods of academic challenge for grieving children. The goal is to reassure parents that their children are getting appropriate support, not simply to suggest that there is a problem parents must address.

GUIDANCE ABOUT FUNERALS

It is important for children to be offered the opportunity to participate in funeral and memorial services. In most cases, it is better for children when they do attend these services. The subject of funerals is discussed in detail in Chapter 3.

Parents may ask teachers for guidance about whether their children should attend funerals. Teachers may be the only professionals who interact with the parents or have the opportunity to provide such advice before the funeral occurs. Teachers can play a valuable role in helping parents understand why this can be so important to children's grieving and ongoing recovery after a death.

CHECKING IN WITH PARENTS

Children in bereavement are coping with many challenges as they make the effort to understand what has happened in their lives. When family members are also struggling, this can create challenges for children. The death of a family member can result in depression in a parent, increases in fighting or domestic violence, financial stresses, and other problems.

Teacher–parent conversations offer an opportunity to see how well the parents and the family are doing as a whole. When the person who died was also important to the parent or parents—and this is typically the case when children lose a family member—they will also be struggling with grief.

Sometimes a teacher's window into a family reveals valuable information that has been missed by others. Teachers may learn that a parent is not coping well,[2] the house is in chaos, the family does not have money for food, or the family has relocated to the overly crowded apartment of an extended family member. They may see ways that the family's response to the death is creating problems for the children. Although teachers cannot personally solve such problems, they can help arrange referrals and support for a troubled family. This can be a great help to students.

AN OPEN INVITATION

Grief is not a quick process. Children who have lost a family member or friend will feel the effects strongly for some time. The trajectory of grief is different for every child, and how this influences school and family life will also be different.

Some children go through an acute period of grief and gradually feel better over time. Others do well for a period of time and face challenges later. Some have a difficult period, do better for a period, and then have difficulties again. When children are struggling, issues may come up at school or at home. The signs might be falling academic performance, troubled social relationships, or increasing conflicts with parents and family.

When teachers talk with parents about grieving children, it is important to leave the door open for additional talks in the future. Both teachers and parents have important information about how children are coping. Their willingness to share these observations can help children over time in all the domains of their lives.

ONGOING CONTACT WITH FAMILIES

Chapter 5 describes ways teachers can make initial contact with families after a death, often by telephone. The goal of this first call is simply to express your condolences, let the family know that they are in your thoughts, and answer any immediate questions they may have, such as about funeral attendance. This is usually the most a parent is ready for immediately following a death.

At a later point, often after students have returned to school, teachers can make contact again. In this instance, the goal is to talk with the parent or parents about how their child is doing in school. The following are some suggestions about what to say and do when meeting parents:

- *Make it personal.* Ideally, teachers and parents can meet face-to-face. When this is not possible, telephone contact can be made. Although some people are quite comfortable with e-mail and instant messaging, we do not recommend this, at least for an initial meeting. There is a great deal of nuance in discussions about grief, and it is easy to miss something essential or miscommunicate with these formats.

- *Normalize the contact.* Teachers should explain that it is a good idea for teachers and parents to meet any time a child experiences the death of a family member or friend. This allows teachers and parents to work together to offer the best possible support for children during this difficult period.

- *Focus on academic and social issues.* Teachers should let the parents know that their interest is in both the child's academic performance and social and emotional health.

- *Let parents know that they are helping the teacher.* During this conversation, teachers will be able to draw information from parents that helps teachers make the best plan for the child. Parents have something valuable to offer.

The timing of these meetings will vary from one family to another. Most families will be grateful to hear from their children's teacher. Many will feel relieved that the teacher is expressing concern and interest. Some parents will be eager to come in and talk about these matters right away. Others may feel too overwhelmed and need more time before they can manage such a meeting. Even when everything is done well, some parents may still prefer to keep their family's loss private and not accept a teacher's assistance.

It is important to respect parents' wishes if they are unable to meet; however, it is also helpful and appropriate to continue to make contact with grieving families over time and to make additional efforts to set up a meeting. If a parent declines the offer to meet, the teacher should leave the door open for further contact if possible. The teacher might say, "I'd just like to check back in a week or so and see if it might work better at that point. I do really want to be sure I'm giving your daughter as much help as I can."

DIFFERENT OUTCOMES

Because every family is different, it is impossible to predict with any certainty what will happen when teachers and families talk. At the NCSCB, we have generally seen positive outcomes from these meetings, and we recommend them highly. However, there can be challenges.

When It Does Not "Work"

It is no surprise to teachers that some of their students live in difficult circumstances, and some of the parenting they receive is less than ideal. These problems can feel especially acute in the context of grief and loss. A struggling family struggles even more. A child who has already been dealing with hardship is dealing with even more.

Sometimes parents do not acknowledge or address their children's needs around bereavement. They may insist that their children are doing fine and do not need any special attention. They may be unable to acknowledge their children's needs because they are too distracted by their own. Some parents have personality or mental health issues, or they are dealing with alcohol or other substance abuse problems that make it difficult for them to ever consider their children's needs in depth.

Sometimes parents simply do not know *how* to address children's needs about grief. They may come from cultures where death is not discussed openly. They may have lived a protected or untroubled life and, therefore, they may be facing complex challenges for the first time. Their spouse may have been the one to handle the "emotional" things, and if that is the person who died, they may feel at a complete loss.

Parents may also have a different belief about what is the right thing to do. They may believe their children can cope with the challenges of grief entirely through prayer and religious observances. They may believe that indulging children's emotions at times such as these makes them weak. They may believe, despite evidence to the contrary, that children do not feel these matters deeply and do not need any special consideration.

We have also seen instances where parents make decisions about what to tell their children that are not helpful. They may denigrate the dead, criticizing a parent who suffered a drug overdose or died in a car crash while speeding. They may obscure the truth, refusing to describe how a family member died. We have known parents who felt unable to tell their children that a sister or brother had died, and they instead carried on a pretense that the child was in the hospital and would come home again.

These are challenging situations. The best course a teacher can take is to continue to strive to make an alliance with such families. If teachers suggest that these parents do not have their children's best interest at heart, a positive alliance will not be possible. In most cases, such parents *are* greatly concerned about their children, but do not know how to meet their needs or feel unable to do so. Teachers who can create an alliance with a family may be able to provide gentle guidance to parents in some of these situations. They can emphasize, with the authority of their expertise as well as their compassion for the family's situation, the importance of telling children the truth.

There may also be instances in which families are simply unwilling to participate in teacher–parent conferences. After making several offers to meet, teachers may have to let go of their intentions to set up a conference.

The best guidelines in these situations are familiar to teachers: Keep trying to do what you know works best for students and be willing to step back when you hit the limits of what you can do. After some time has passed and the parents have started to adjust to the loss or come to realize the distress their children are experiencing, they may be ready to accept the teacher's offer to meet.

Of course, any time a teacher has reasonable suspicion or evidence that neglect or abuse is occurring, a report to the proper authorities is necessary. This is true even for a family struggling with recent grief.

When It Does "Work"

Teacher–parent conferences that "work" are not necessarily easy encounters either. Grieving parents may express deep feelings of loss, be very emotional, or have some trouble following the conversation. Just like their children and all people who are in acute grief, they are likely to have trouble with concentration and feel overwhelmed.

Parents who become engaged in these conversations may also pose some difficult questions. However, this can actually be a sign of success—parents are interested, involved, and concerned. They are looking for guidance and willing to hear suggestions. For example, families often describe some dilemma or question about their child and then look to the teacher for an answer—"What would you do if it was your child?"

In general matters, such as whether to tell the truth about a death or let a child attend a funeral, teachers can safely offer appropriate guidance. "I think you can trust that your child is able to hear the truth about this death, and that will be the healthiest thing." In more complex situations, however, it becomes necessary to reflect the question back to the parents. For example, a grieving mother says her 10-year-old son, whose father died 2 weeks ago, has decided he wants to spend his entire summer with his grandparents. In a situation such as this, the best course is to help the mother continue to assess the situation so that she can make a good decision. A helpful response might be, "I don't really know all of the concerns in your family and with your child, so I can't make the best judgments. But let's talk about what you feel you should do."

Giving parents an opportunity to engage in these types of discussions can be helpful to them, to their family, and to grieving students. Teachers can model how to engage in gentle, frank conversations about death. They can show respect for the range of feelings and responses parents are having, and they can show compassion for the concerns they experience for their children. They can reassure them that a wide range of responses to death are common, and they can offer resources for additional support.

All of these steps reinforce the importance of parents in their children's lives and the power of their relationships. There is probably no other time in the lives of children when it is more important for parents to understand how vital and essential they are to their children's success and well-being.

ENDNOTES

1. *After a Loved One Dies—How Children Grieve and How Parents and Other Adults Can Support Them* (Schonfeld & Quackenbush, 2009) is a free resource for families that follows the same guidelines as this book. It can be downloaded or ordered in hardcopy for the cost of shipping and handling only. See the References section for full information. Another excellent resource for parents to help their children and themselves after the death of a family member is *Guiding Your Child Through Grief* (Emswiler & Emswiler, 2000).
2. Krell and Rabkin (1979) present a model of how parental guilt after a death can significantly alter family dynamics and how parents interact with surviving siblings.

7

Special Concerns for Bereaved Children

Mourning a death is a challenge for any child. Some children, however, have additional circumstances that make this process even more complicated. Circumstances of the death or characteristics of the family may complicate matters. Some children have difficulties understanding or otherwise making sense of the events. This can make it even harder to move forward through the grieving process.

When teachers recognize students in bereavement, acknowledge their loss, and make themselves available for ongoing conversations or contact, they offer immensely valuable support. For students with additional challenges, teachers and school mental health professionals may need to guide their families to other resources, such as a bereavement counselor or mental health provider, to make sure those children have the support they need.

COMPLICATED MOURNING

Although mourning is often a complex and difficult process, there is usually a sense of transition over time. In the first days after a death, surviving family members and friends often ride a roller coaster of emotions. They might sob uncontrollably at one point, feel empty and without emotion 20 minutes later, share fond memories and laughter an hour after that, and then begin sobbing deeply again.

A week or two after the death, they might be having similar responses, but there is a sense of change and movement. The deep sobbing might still occur, but less often. Although the exact features of grief are not the same from person to person, the sense that they gradually shift and change is common. Usually, some months after the death, the feelings of grief have less intensity, although they often continue to be strong.

In some situations, however, people seem to "get stuck" at one particular, difficult point of the mourning process. Instead of gradual improvement, the situation may become increasingly difficult. That is, the feeling of positive movement—of change or progress—is still absent months after the death. Individuals may also demonstrate unusual or particularly severe reactions, such as intense guilt. They may be unable to draw on inner resources or external support. They cannot adjust to the new reality of life without their loved one. Mental health providers call this *complicated mourning*.[1]

What Complicated Mourning Looks Like

At first, complicated mourning may look like any other mourning process. It is the degree or nature of reactions, the extent to which they persist, and the fact that they sometimes get worse instead of better that are striking. People suffering from complicated grief might experience any of the following:

- *They may not move forward in their grief process.* The loss of a close family member or friend often brings ongoing feelings of sadness or despair. At first, it may be difficult for grieving people to imagine ever enjoying life again. Over time, they find some things that bring moments of pleasure—a beautiful sunset, a funny movie, a dinner with family and friends. As time moves forward and the death is increasingly distant, they find the moments of despair happen less frequently and the moments of enjoyment occur more often.

  In complicated mourning, this shift in the pattern of sadness and enjoyment may not occur. Each day may feel as difficult as the first day of grief, and this continues over a period of months or even years.

- *They may have difficulty managing the ongoing responsibilities of their lives.* Over time, most grieving people are gradually able to resume the responsibilities in their lives. For children, this would include school and perhaps other activities, such as working at an after-school job (for older students); helping out with household chores; or participating in clubs, sports, or other extracurricular activities. For adults, this usually includes work or caring for children or other family members. They keep gas in the car and food in the kitchen (most of the time). The house gets cleaned (perhaps not as thoroughly as before), and the lawn gets mowed (at least occasionally).

  In complicated mourning, these responsibilities may continue to feel overwhelming. Children continue to have difficulty concentrating in school. They may not be interested in other activities, or they may find they simply cannot do what they once did easily—pass a football, play a song on their guitar, or sit through a club meeting or religious service.

- *They have problems with social connections.* In acute grief, some people push away friends or family for a period of time. They may feel like no one can understand what they are going through. They may question the meaning or purpose of their relationships and the social activities they used to enjoy. Children may be confused about the ways their own feelings have changed and feel unsure about how to act around family or friends. This is one of the reasons grief can be isolating. Over time, however, grieving children and adults who have experienced this kind of isolation find their way back to social connections that have meaning for them. Some of their relationships may change, but they find they can feel close to people again.

In complicated mourning, people may isolate themselves from many or all of their friends and family in an ongoing way. The relationships do not improve after a few weeks or months. They resist the attempts people make to spend time with them.

- *They cannot stop thinking about the deceased.* When we first lose people we love, they are in our thoughts constantly. "She would have loved this movie." "He will never get to ride his bicycle along this beautiful road again." "This party would be great if only she were here." Sometimes, it may feel as if we cannot get away from such thoughts. They intrude on everything we do.

   Over time, these thoughts usually continue, but they are less frequent and less intrusive. We miss our loved one, but still can have a pretty good time at the party. We think of him when we walk along his favorite country road, and we are able to truly enjoy the beauty for ourselves. We know how much she would have enjoyed this book or movie or television show, and we can go ahead and enjoy it as well.

   In complicated mourning, it may be difficult or impossible to enjoy life. Thoughts of the deceased are constantly present, and the person's grief is relentless. Disturbing images of the loved one at the moment of death may intrude repeatedly. Longing for the deceased is powerful, and survivors may have difficulty accepting the fact of the death. There is no hope, no bright moment, no satisfaction or happiness. The absence of the loved one taints everything.

- *They may abuse alcohol or other drugs.* Sometimes, people who are grieving find themselves turning to alcohol or other drugs more than they did before the death. They may be trying to calm their nerves, get some sleep, or numb their pain. Eventually, most will realize that substance use is not helping them cope with their grief, and their use will drop back to previous levels.

   In complicated mourning, people may continue to use substances more frequently. They may abuse prescription medicines. Problems with use may worsen over time, and they may show signs of a substance abuse disorder. Although younger children do not often abuse substances, adolescents experiencing complicated mourning may.

- *They may have persistent thoughts of suicide.* Many people who lose a loved one have moments when they wonder whether life is still worth living. They cannot picture themselves ever feeling happiness again. They may imagine or believe that their own death will allow them to see their loved one again. If these thoughts occur, they are usually transient—they come and go. As with most symptoms of grief, they tend to be more common early in the process and become less common over time. There are likely to be "thinking about it" moments, rather than persistent and troubling thoughts of suicide.

   In complicated mourning, when thoughts of suicide occur, they are more likely to be persistent and have great force. This might include making specific plans, such as how and when the suicide will take place. People experiencing this kind of grief may actually begin to follow through on their planning, perhaps taking steps to put their affairs in order or think about when and how they will do this. This level of planning and preparation is an unusual response to grief and represents a psychiatric emergency. Care is required immediately, even if the person is reluctant to seek help or resists doing so.

• *Emotional, mental health, or learning problems present before the death worsen significantly.* People coping with the stress of grief often experience difficulties with preexisting conditions. These additional challenges can range from mild to severe. For example, people who had mild and occasional anxiety or blue moods before the death might find they have anxiety or depression serious enough to warrant treatment. People who have had moderate depression for some time that was treated successfully with therapy or antidepressants may find themselves dealing with more complicated symptoms that no longer respond well to their existing treatment. They may need to try new medications or receive therapy more frequently for a period of time.

  Children may develop, or experience, a worsening of many different conditions. These include such things as anxiety, depression, school refusal, oppositional disorders, attention problems (i.e., attention-deficit/hyperactivity disorder), or obsessive compulsive disorder. They may need special attention and additional support to cope with these challenges for some period after the death.

  In complicated mourning, the worsening of problems is dramatic in some way. The symptoms become much more severe, or they do not respond to usual supports and assistance.

Often, children who are experiencing complicated mourning show typical symptoms of depression. These might include such symtoms as irritability or anger, feelings of hopelessness, or withdrawal from family and friends. Children may show either an increase or decrease in appetite and begin sleeping much more, or much less, than usual. Difficulty concentrating and physical complaints, such as stomachaches, may also occur. Feelings of guilt are common, and feelings of worthlessness and thoughts of suicide sometimes emerge.

Children who have a parent experiencing complicated mourning are facing tremendous burdens. They fear for their parent's welfare. Their home life may become disorganized because essential household tasks are not getting done. At a time when they most need emotional support and reassurance, they have a parent who is unable to give it to them. It can be devastating for a child to realize that all he or she has to offer is not enough to make a parent let go of the grief and "come back" to the world.

Intervention is recommended for children and adults who suffer from complicated mourning. In many cases, a combination of therapy and medication helps people work through their difficulties and begin to move forward in the process of grieving. It is quite important that parents experiencing complicated mourning get treatment or intervention so they are better able to care for their children.

Even when children suffering from complicated mourning are referred for mental health services, the role of teachers in offering support is important. Teachers play a unique role in children's lives. Mental health providers cannot duplicate this—they offer a different type of support. The comfort children receive from a caring, concerned teacher continues to be meaningful and valuable to children, even in these most difficult circumstances.

When Complicated Mourning Is More Likely

Anyone might experience complicated mourning. This can occur for children and adults who have excellent social support, strong coping skills, and no previous history of emotional difficulty. However, there are factors that make complicated mourning more likely for children.[2] As with many other elements of grieving, these include circumstances of the death and circumstances in the lives of the students and their families.

Circumstances of the Death

No death is easy, but some deaths are more difficult to understand or imagine— why it happened, how it happened, why it happened to this person. The following are seven examples of deaths that may lead to complicated mourning:

- *Deaths caused by traumatic circumstances.* Deaths due to traumatic circumstances usually occur suddenly. They often involve significant elements of "bad luck" or fate. For example, if the person had not been standing on that particular corner, if the driver of the car had left home 60 seconds later, or if someone else had been on call that night the death would not have occurred. These are often deaths that are also painful to imagine. The deceased might have suffered. There may have been disfigurement or mutilation of the body. The person may have been alone at the moment of death.

- *Deaths by violence.* Violent deaths are a particularly difficult form of traumatic loss. Similar to other deaths by trauma, it is painful to imagine the moment of death and the effects on the body.

Living with Grief and Fear

Kendra, a 9-year-old girl, lived in a large city with her mother, Laurette. Laurette worked as a bartender and occasionally dated men she met at the bar. She didn't always show the best judgment about men. One of her former partners was a man with a history of violence, and Kendra watched in horror one day when he threatened to kill her mother. He turned to Kendra and said, "And I'll kill you, too."

One evening about a year later, Laurette came home after work to an impatient daughter complaining that they were out of cat food and that her mother needed to go buy some *now*. Laurette sighed, picked up her purse, and headed out to the local convenience store. She didn't return to the apartment, and after several anxious hours, Kendra called an aunt who lived in another state.

The aunt called the authorities in Laurette's town and learned that her sister had been shot and killed in the parking lot of the convenience store.

The aunt called Kendra's grandfather, who lived near Laurette's apartment. He came over immediately, had Kendra pack a bag, and drove off with her to her aunt and uncle's home. There, she was informed of the tragic circumstances of her mother's death. She never returned to the apartment she'd shared with her mother.

Kendra's aunt and uncle took custody of her. This was a difficult transition for her. Her relatives lived a quiet life with structure and rules that were unfamiliar to her. She missed her old independence.

She was not allowed to attend her mother's funeral. She had not taken any mementos from the apartment and had nothing of her mother's to remember her by. The entire family was vague about the details of the death. They seemed embarrassed about how Laurette lived her life and the fact that she was murdered. They believed it was better to focus on the future rather than dwell on the past.

Kendra was furious about the way she was being treated, and she acted in ways that showed this. She was disrespectful to her aunt and uncle. She refused to follow their rules. She didn't want the new clothes they bought her. Sometimes she cursed at them. "In this house," they told her, "we insist on respect."

"No one is respecting me!" she shouted back. "No one will tell me anything! You're treating me like a little kid."

She began acting out at her new school, creating disturbances in the classroom and conflicts with her classmates. She didn't want to make new friends. She didn't want to learn new things. She refused to talk about her past life. Her teacher reported that she often seemed anxious and distracted.

It was clear that something needed to be done for Kendra, so she was referred for counseling. The counselor asked her if she would talk about some of the things on her mind. Kendra told him she worried that she would be murdered just as her mother was. At first, this seemed to be an understandable reaction to the circumstances of her mother's death, but as Kendra continued to talk, the counselor realized that there was more to the story. Kendra believed her mother had been murdered by the man who had threatened them both. She was living in terrible fear that he would track her down. Sometimes, she believed she saw him in crowds searching for her.

The counselor spoke with the family about Kendra's concerns. They were surprised to hear this story. Kendra was able to give identifying information about the man who had made the threats, and the police were able to locate him. He had been arrested before Laurette's murder and had been in custody since that time. He was not a suspect in her mother's murder.

Kendra's family began to talk to her more about her mother and what the police were doing to find the murderer. She was reassured that this was someone who did not know her and could never find her. As they continued these conversations, they were able to talk with her about other thoughts and feelings she was having about her mother.

The counselor met with Kendra again, and they talked more about her mother. Kendra complained that she had not been able to take any of her mother's possessions. She didn't have any of their family photographs. If she'd had the chance, she would have taken along some of her mother's shirts, one of her bottles of perfume, and a stuffed animal her mom kept on the bed.

Laurette's apartment had not been emptied yet, so other family members were able to gather some mementos for Kendra. She received a package with some of her mother's possessions, as well as the family photos. These remembrances meant a great deal to Kendra.

Her aunt and uncle took Kendra to visit her mother's gravesite. Although she was still upset that she had missed the funeral, this at least gave her an opportunity to say goodbye to her mother. She made her aunt and uncle promise they would bring her back again in the future. They readily agreed once they realized how important this was to Kendra.

After this, Kendra didn't feel she needed to talk further with the counselor. By now, the family was being more open with Kendra, and she responded well to their greater honesty. She began to follow the family rules more successfully, and sometimes responded to their efforts to show affection. She calmed down in school and began to apply herself to her classes.

One day, her uncle invited her to the school's father–daughter dance. Kendra snorted. "You can't be serious," she said. "What a stupid idea." After a while, though, she changed her mind and told her uncle that she would like to go. They both enjoyed the event, and it was the beginning of a time of increasing closeness for all of them. Once Kendra was reassured about her own safety and could trust her aunt and uncle to be honest with her, she moved on in her grieving and was able to adjust successfully to her new life.

- *Deaths that are not socially sanctioned or whose impact is not appreciated.* Some deaths are more troublesome socially, and people may find it more difficult to talk about them. They may not know what to say to survivors. Gossip or rumors may surround such deaths. Bereaved family members may experience a sense of shame. As a result, survivors may not ask for or receive the same level of support they might for other types of deaths.

  These might include deaths from suicide, certain diseases (e.g., AIDS), or drug- or alcohol-related causes. The grief of survivors when someone dies while committing an act of violence is another area that may not be acknowledged. Children are sensitive to the stigma surrounding such deaths and may be more hesitant than usual to acknowledge their feelings or seek support.

  People may underestimate the impact of a death on someone when they do not understand the personal connection of the survivor to the deceased.

Deaths of an estranged former spouse or miscarriages early in pregnancy often result in far more impact than friends or colleagues realize. Survivors may grieve with limited social support. Deaths of stepchildren or half-siblings who spent most of their time with another family may not be recognized in the same way as the death of someone who always lived with the family.

- *Sudden deaths.* When deaths are sudden and unexpected, the pain of loss is not necessarily greater; however, the shock of it can be traumatic and can interfere with the usual processes of grief.

- *Deaths after a long illness.* Long illnesses place immense burdens on families. The person who is ill may deteriorate slowly over a period of years while the family struggles to provide care. Financial circumstances often become challenging. The person who is ill may be irritable and difficult, and the physical and mental processes of decline can be agonizing to witness.

    Even in the most loving families, people going through these experiences find themselves wishing, at times, that death would be hastened. They do not wish to see a loved one suffer and, while people talk about this less often, people sometimes wish to be relieved from their own suffering related to the demands of the illness. Confusing feelings of guilt, relief, regret, and sadness are not at all unusual in such circumstances, and, when strong, these may contribute to episodes of complicated mourning.

- *Deaths seen as preventable.* Sometimes a death seems preventable. If someone had continued talking with a loved one for 30 seconds longer, the person would not have been hit by the truck. If a family member had decided to take the person to the emergency room a few hours earlier, doctors might have saved his life. Sometimes, these impressions have some basis in fact—if the seatbelt had been fastened, if the medication had been given properly, or if the mother had never gotten involved with the violent boyfriend, then death might have been averted. Powerful feelings of guilt contribute to the risk for complicated mourning.

- *Public deaths.* When deaths receive public attention for any reason, children and families may face special challenges in coping. Sometimes the recognition is positive—a family member may have died a hero for saving someone or died while in military service. Other times, the attention may be about more troubling matters—a family member died during a crime or in macabre circumstances.

    The additional attention these deaths receive places burdens on children. Other people have their own ideas and attitudes about what occurred, and children are likely to hear comments from peers and adults. Disturbing posts or images may appear on Internet sites.

    There is less of a sense of privacy about these deaths and the process of grieving. Survivors may find themselves in the public eye much of the time. They may feel embarrassed about how they are reacting to the death and worry that they are not living up to what society and peers expect of them.

They may be ashamed if they cry in public or worried that if they do not cry, people will question how much they cared about the deceased.

There may be public demands on the family, such as appearances at communitywide memorial services. Children may not see the events the same way that those from the community do. They may not feel grateful that their father was a hero, for example, but angry that he put himself at risk and abandoned the family by dying.

Circumstances of the Student or Family

A number of family or individual circumstances can increase the risk for complicated mourning. The following are several examples of these situations:

- *Emotional problems.* Children with current emotional problems, or those with a previous history of problems, are more likely to have complicated grief reactions. Typical problems include such things as anxiety disorders or depression. In addition, some children have family members with emotional or mental health problems. This can also increase risk for complicated grief reactions among children or their family.

- *Ambivalent relationship with the deceased.* Some children are ambivalent about family members who die. They may have lost a mother who abandoned the family when they were very young. The person who died may have abused them in some way. They may have felt jealous of the person. They may have been in a developmental period in which they were struggling for more independence and resented a parent's limits or restrictions. They may gain benefits as a result of the death, such as greater status within the family or more freedom or respect.

  These ambivalent feelings are difficult. Children may feel relieved or indifferent about the death. They may have true and deep feelings of loss as well as confusing feelings of satisfaction. When such dissonant feelings occur, complicated mourning is more likely.

- *Struggles for autonomy and independence.* High school students have begun to break away from their parents in anticipation of leaving the family home for college or work. At some level, most long for freedom. Often, teens resent adult supervision and the restrictions in their lives. Many families go through periods of turmoil related to adolescent rebellion or the struggle for autonomy. However, as adolescents move through these times of transition, they typically also have periods where they want and need to approach their parents for advice and support. Those who have left the family home still look forward to return visits. Although they may seem "ready" and even eager to leave their parents, a parent's death in late adolescence can be a particularly stressful loss.

- *Unusually intense or dependent relationship with the deceased.* Some children may have had an unusually close or intense relationship with the person who died. This might have been an especially dependent relationship, such as is typical in a young preschool child. It might have been a relationship that offered important support that was not available from others, such as a deaf child who lost the only person in the family who understood and used sign language. For some children, the person who died may have been the safe relationship in a family storm—a grandmother who provided a haven from physical or sexual abuse by the mother's boyfriend, or an aunt who always helped get the schizophrenic father to the hospital when he decompensated. Losing someone so essential to everyday survival can contribute to the risk for complicated mourning.

- *History of other losses or stressors.* Children who experience loss, even when it involves the death of a close family member, are usually fairly resilient. When they can turn to others for support and guidance, they usually learn to cope and move forward. However, when children go through multiple losses over time or experience other serious stressors, the response to new stressors, including grief, can be more difficult.

  This encompasses a wide range of possible circumstances. A child who has already lost one parent, for example, will have a much more difficult time losing a second parent. Children who have been emotionally, physically, or sexually abused have lost much of their innate resilience. Children who have already been witness to death and loss (e.g., coming from a war-torn country, growing up in an urban area where they have lost classmates and family members to violence) have already spent many of the natural resources they were given. Cumulative loss of any type can increase the risk of complicated mourning.

- *Lack of social support.* Grief is both an intensely personal and a social process. It is important for people who are grieving to receive support from others. Grieving children need touch, reassurance, a listening ear, patience, and acceptance. These are not things they can get on their own—they must be delivered by another human being.

  Some children do not receive this kind of support. Their families may be incapable of offering it, and they may not have strong relationships with peers. They may be the quiet kids at school who do not cause problems, do not stand out, and do not receive much attention. They may not give any indication that they need or want such support—indeed, they may not be aware themselves that they need it. Children who have little or no social support are more likely to experience complicated mourning.

DEATH AND SECONDARY LOSS

Another factor that can make it harder to adjust to the death of a loved one is secondary loss. When children lose someone close to them, they experience the immediate and direct effects of that death. In most instances, especially if the deceased is a parent or primary caregiver, they also experience additional losses in their lives. Examples of secondary loss include the following:

- *Changed relationships.* When people die, they leave behind a circle of work associates, friends, and family members. Children have their own place in this circle and often enjoy the relationships within it. However, the deceased was the center of that circle, and when the center is gone, the circle itself may dissolve.

Even when children receive support about the loss of a family member or friend, they may not receive support about the loss of these relationships. They no longer get the special attention from the secretary at their mother's office. Their aunt and uncle do not come by much any more now that their father has died. Their brother's friend who used to come over and play guitar, teaching them a few chords along the way, no longer drops by.

Sometimes, relationships that seem fairly incidental to adults have tremendous importance to children. This is especially true for children who have limited support in other ways or who are dealing with family problems.

- *Moving.* When a parent or other family member dies, the family may have to move. A move to a new neighborhood, city, or state can create a stressful transition for children who are already grieving. After the death of a family member, it often seems as if everything about the world has changed. When children must also relocate, this becomes literally true. In addition to this death, they also lose familiar places, their school, and their friends.

- *Lifestyle.* When a parent or other source of financial support for a family dies, the family's financial circumstances often change. Families can lose their homes, their sense of financial security, their ability to fund their children's college education, and their ability to comfortably purchase other things they want or need. Surviving parents may need to work more hours or at a more demanding job and, therefore, be less available at a time when children especially need their presence and support.

Some families must move into smaller, less expensive living spaces. They may move from a single-family home to an apartment, or from a three-bedroom apartment to a one-room place, which may mean less privacy, more crowding, and, usually, more family tension.

In some instances, children may also experience a distinct shift in class or social status after the death of a parent. They may not be able to participate in special school programs that involve extra costs. They may need to purchase secondhand clothing for the first time in their lives. They might suddenly become eligible for subsidized school lunch programs. All of these changes can add additional layers of emotion, such as shame, anger, or sadness, to the grief they are already experiencing.

- *Peer group status.* Children may also experience shifts in peer group status related to some of these changes. If they move to another area, they must reestablish themselves in a new peer group. If a popular friend died, it may disrupt their connections to others in their circle of friends. If they lose financial resources, they may no longer be accepted or feel comfortable in their former peer group. If their family member or friend died with some taint of scandal, they may withdraw from their friends or be avoided by them.

Although, as adults, we would like to think that issues of status are not important at such times, children and teens can be quite sensitive to these matters. For some children, the shift in status will be substantial.

- *Shared memories.* Families share important memories—"The day you were born," "The mischief you used to get into when you were a toddler," "Your first day of school." Children love to hear these stories told and retold as they grow up. The stories make them feel special, and they help affirm their sense of place in the family. They provide a sense of continuity as new memories and stories are woven in over time. Sometimes, new bits of information come out—"One time, you were going to get punished by Grandma because of your mischief, but she just couldn't stop laughing."

  It is an extraordinarily powerful experience to have someone hold this special set of memories about you—the unique, singular person you are. Therefore, when children lose someone who has these kinds of memories about them, they lose a thread to their own sense of self. No one else knows them in quite that way, and no one else will ever know them in quite that way again.

- *Shared visions and plans for the future.* Although most children are strongly oriented to the present, they also have plans for the future. Their family members are part of those plans. When a family member dies, these visions change. Will graduating from eighth grade mean as much if the parent or grandparent is not there to see it? Will the swim meet next month matter? How will a student choose a college or complete applications without this person's support? What about the planned drive down the coast or the imagined trip to Hawaii? Children have many things in the forefront or background of their minds that can be affected by a death.

- *A sense of security and safety.* In our daily lives, we tend to make certain assumptions. We probably assume, for example, that we will walk out of our door in the morning as we always do and go to work, see our colleagues, have lunch, and perhaps take a little walk. We assume that we will come back to our home after work and find it intact. We expect to see our family members for dinner and have conversations in the evening as we always do.

  This is called the *assumptive world.*[3] These are the things we automatically count on; they are part of the background in our lives. Generally, it is good to be able to make these assumptions. This frees up our attention so we can focus on the things that are changing every day in our lives—a new project at work, a bill that needs to be paid, a special visit with an old friend. It allows us to go through our day without becoming overwhelmed with all of the tragedies that *could* occur.

  When children or adults experience a death, they experience the loss of this assumptive world. They assumed, before this event, that they would see their family member or friend again. They then realize that much of what they had taken for granted was really an assumption. Now, because this person has died, they lose their ability to trust any of the assumptions they make.

Children sometimes feel this loss more acutely than adults who have already had experiences with death. How can they trust that they will see any of the people they love again? How do they know that they will not die as their family member or friend did? How can they be sure that anything will ever feel normal again? This loss of an everyday presumption of safety and security can lead to feelings of vulnerability and anxiety. People grieve not only the death but also the loss of their ability to trust that things—almost anything—will be okay.

Making Grief More Challenging

These experiences of secondary loss reinforce the primary grief experience. A young girl who has lost her father is struggling to regain some sense of normalcy in her life, but every day she is reminded of his absence by the crowded conditions of the new, small apartment where her family had to move. A young man who has been planning to go to college cannot stop thinking about his mother's death because he cannot imagine how to make his decisions, or finance his education, without her. An 8-year-old boy whose favorite aunt has died wonders who will tell him at his next birthday about all of the things they did together when he visited her farm, the way she had done as far back as he can remember. When secondary loss experiences are powerful and lasting, mourning may become complicated.

Way Too Many Changes

Eight-year-old Dylan's mother died after a long struggle with cancer. One way his father coped with all of the painful memories of his life during her illness was to change things. He bought a new car. He switched jobs. He moved the family to a new home. Then he met and began dating a new woman. Within a year of his first wife's death, he had remarried.

Dylan found all of the changes unsettling. He had to adjust to a new school and new friends, and now there was a new woman living in his home. He had trouble accepting his father's new wife as a part of the family so quickly, even though he liked her. He told his counselor, "He treats her like she's a queen. I mean, she shouldn't just be a maid, but she shouldn't be a queen, either. She should be somewhere in between."

Dylan had a number of reasonable and appropriate issues related to grief about his mother's death, but all of these were worsened by the extraordinary number of secondary losses he experienced.

Grief and Students in Transition

Students go through many transitions in their lives. They may begin with preschool and then move to elementary school. They graduate to middle school. They move on to high school, and then perhaps college, trade school, or the military.

Young people often experience other transitions as well. A divorce can change the configuration of their family. A job transfer may mean the family moves to a new state. An aging grandparent may move into the house, or an older sister may move out.

Children are more vulnerable during times of transition. They are more likely to start new, risky behaviors, such as smoking, drinking, or drug use. Experiencing a death around the time of a transition can make grieving more difficult. In addition, transitions are also times when grief issues from an earlier loss may reemerge. For example, a child who lost a parent while in third grade and then had some school difficulties may have received support, gotten back on track, and returned to satisfactory school work. However, when he moves to a new school in seventh grade, he has to shift classrooms several times a day and is no longer in the company of familiar classmates and teachers. He then begins to have school problems again.

Students may also feel heightened effects of bereavement during their high school years when academic performance becomes especially important. College-bound students in particular feel pressure about GPAs, advanced placement classes, and SAT scores. They want to develop effective interview skills. Some are making extraordinary efforts to build résumés for college applications by participating in school clubs, doing volunteer work, or taking on other extracurricular activities.

These endeavors are stressful for any student. For bereaved students, they may be especially challenging. They may be unable to perform at their best if they have experienced a recent loss. The heightened pressures of this time can also bring up difficulties related to earlier losses.

Students are also sensitive to the statements made by family members after a loss. Older students often take on additional responsibilities in the family if a parent has died. They may help younger children with homework, do grocery shopping, drive siblings to their baseball games, and keep the lawn mowed. They may also be providing emotional support to surviving parents—talking to them late at night, encouraging them to return to social activities, offering a shoulder to cry on. If the surviving parent becomes dependent on this support, it is more difficult for the student to make a transition to college, especially if this means leaving the area. A parent who says, "Your help has been wonderful, and I am so grateful for all you have done," is expressing important appreciation. However, if that parent adds, "I could never do this without you," it makes leaving for college even more difficult.

Some of these students will change their plans and choose to attend nearby colleges that allow them to stay geographically close to their families. Some will go away to college and find that they are unable to tolerate the distance from their families. These students may drop out so they can return to their family home.

Sometimes, postponing independence from the family is what works best for the student and the family. This may be a time when it feels right for everyone to be close together. It is important, however, to support young people in making independent choices about these matters. If they stay close to their family because they feel enmeshed and unable to free themselves from the burden of their family's grief, it will not be a helpful course of action for anyone in the family. Such students may develop feelings of resentment, frustration, guilt, or shame, or they may experience symptoms of complicated mourning or other emotional problems. (Additional issues regarding transitions are discussed in Chapter 8.)

Students with Special Needs

Students with special needs or disabilities are as unique as students who are typically developing, and there are no hard-and-fast rules that apply to all of them. When students with learning and/or developmental disabilities experience the death of a family member or friend, however, it is likely that they will need more reassurance, patience, and understanding than other children.

Death challenges most people's understanding. Adults as well as children may not initially understand what has happened, or they may need to hear information more than once. Younger children are especially likely to need repeated explanations about such things as the Four Concepts About Death, what happened to the deceased, how their own lives might change, what kind of support they can ask for, and where they can receive support.

These issues are often simply a matter of degree with students with intellectual and social-emotional disabilities. They may ask the same questions many times. They may want to listen to an explanation many times. Students may hear an explanation, accept it, and then decide later that they still are not quite sure what it means. Concrete examples are usually helpful, and conversations about the meaning of death and their relationship with the deceased may be revisited often.

School communications with family members are especially important with these students. Teachers will want to offer support in helping students understand what has happened. To do this, they will want to gain a sense of what has been explained already and how the death is being discussed in the family. They may be able to offer guidance to parents and other family members about how to discuss this event. Again, these are basically the same steps recommended for all students, but the extent of discussion may simply be more—just as it is with other topics in their education and their lives.

Parents of children with special needs may also find it particularly upsetting to have discussions about the death. Having to explain in simple and direct terms what the death means and what impact it has on the family, especially repeatedly, is difficult for the parent who is also grieving. If a parent has died, surviving parents may be so worried about what will happen to their child who has special needs if they also die that they may be unable even to begin the conversation.

Special education teachers, or general education teachers who know students well, are often the strongest resource when their students with intellectual or social-emotional disabilities have faced the death of a family member or friend. Teachers are often among the most skilled and trusted communicators in their lives. They are familiar with the concepts that students are likely to grasp easily, as well as those that will be a challenge. They know how the students respond when they are frustrated, frightened, or confused. They have already addressed challenging topics with them, such as difficulties with peers, classroom behavior, emotions, and other sensitive issues.

WHEN MORE IS NEEDED: REFERRING FOR OUTSIDE SERVICES

Many children will benefit from additional services to help them cope with their grief. Children who are experiencing complicated mourning or who have particular challenges related to the loss (such as those outlined in this chapter) that place them at higher risk of complicated mourning, *even if their mourning does not yet appear to be unusual,* are especially likely to need this extra support. It can guide them through the grief process in a manner that helps them continue participating in school and learning. It can also support them as they sustain and build on the existing relationships in their lives.

Signs that children need additional support might include any of the following, particularly when the behaviors are new or become markedly worse than they were before the death:

- *School problems or failure.* Some difficulties with school are common immediately after a death. If they persist, students need further support.

- *Aggressive or delinquent behaviors.* Students may develop new problem behaviors or earlier problem behaviors may worsen.

- *Guilt.* Feelings of guilt are extremely common after a death; however, when they are persistent, marked, or related to a rational sense of responsibility (e.g., when a child drowns while under the supervision of an older sibling), counseling is recommended.

- *Apathy.* Students who were once connected to peers, classroom activities, or school programs may stop feeling that sense of connection and thus become apathetic.

- *Self-destructive behaviors.* Among adolescents, self-destructive behaviors might include new or increased use of alcohol or other drugs, reckless driving, or risky sexual behavior. Younger children might take physical risks, such as jumping off of walls or riding their bicycles dangerously.

- *Social withdrawal or isolation.* Formerly sociable students who no longer seek out interactions with peers may be withdrawing because of a complicated grief reaction.

- *Talk of suicide.* This is always a concern, no matter what the circumstances. Children who talk of suicide should be seen by a mental health professional right away.

Teachers sometimes state that they are not appropriately trained to make assessments about students' mental health. However, teachers are familiar with the personality and performance of specific students, as well as with the behaviors typical of all students. This leaves them in an excellent position to observe students' behaviors and notice when something has changed.

When questions arise about whether a student needs additional support, our general advice is to go ahead and make a referral. Almost all grieving students will benefit from extra attention at this time. If students *are* suffering from complicated mourning, a referral could make a significant difference in their present and future success in school and in their relationships with family and friends.

Getting Susan Back to School

Susan had been looking forward to the school's big basketball game for more than a week. Her good friend Catharine was a cheerleader at the game, and after their school team won, they both were excited. Catharine went out for ice cream with Susan after the game and then returned to Susan's house to spend the night. During the night, Susan thought she heard an odd noise, but she drifted back to sleep. The next morning she woke to find Catharine dead in the bed next to her.

Susan was overwhelmed and felt intensely guilty. Was that noise her friend choking or trying to let her know that she needed help? Was it her fault her friend died? Susan was unable to sleep in her bedroom again after that night. She stayed with another friend, but she wasn't able to sleep. She couldn't talk to her friend or her parents. She withdrew from her mother, despite her mother's repeated attempts to get her to sleep at home again.

Susan had already had some trouble with depression prior to this episode. She had been treated with antidepressants and had seen a psychiatrist for several months. About 6 months earlier, the psychiatrist had moved out of state. Because Susan was doing better, she and her mother decided to stop the medication. She didn't resume counseling with anyone else.

The school, learning of Susan's condition, was very concerned that she was depressed again and worried that she might be suicidal. In order to emphasize the urgency, the principal told her mother that Susan should not return to school until a psychiatrist had completed an evaluation and affirmed she was not at risk of harming herself. Susan didn't want to speak to a doctor and wouldn't return home. Susan's mother called around to psychiatrists in the area, but the first openings she found were a month away or more.

She had no idea what to do next. Fortunately, the school remained in contact with the family to see how she was doing after this incident. They talked with Susan's mother and offered the assistance of a counselor in the school. He made a few calls to mental health professionals he knew in the local community. He was able to get an appointment for Susan to be seen that same day. He understood that she needed to be seen quickly, and he was also eager to help her return to school as soon as possible.

Susan agreed to meet with the psychiatrist because she wanted to get back to school. As it turned out, Susan made a good connection with the psychiatrist and agreed to do a brief course of therapy. The psychiatrist recommended Susan return to school immediately. Susan was, over time, able to manage her anxiety, come to some understanding about what had happened, and come to terms with her guilt. She was eventually able to tolerate being at home with her mother again.

The quick response of the school and the assistance of the school counselor, her mother, and the psychiatrist helped prevent what could have been a much more complicated course of mourning.

Professional Resources

Resources for support include
- School counseling services
- A pediatrician or other health care provider
- Bereavement support groups for families and children
- Community-based mental health services
- Hospice programs

In these more complicated situations, children usually need to be seen by professionals. However, a teacher's or school's awareness and sensitivity to the issues can make an immense difference in a child's ability to get that extra help in a timely and appropriate fashion.

ENDNOTES

1. See Rando (1993) for an excellent textbook for clinicians on the topic of complicated mourning.
2. Several of these factors were highlighted by the Institute of Medicine in their summary of factors associated in the literature with an increased risk of psychological morbidity for children following the death of a parent or sibling. See Osterweis, Solomon, and Green (1984).
3. For further discussion of the assumptive world and the impact of bereavement, see Rando (1993).

8
Providing
Support over Time

Grief changes over time, but for most of us, the death of someone we care about stays with us in some way throughout our lives. This is especially true for children. As they continue to develop and grow, they are able to bring more complex understanding to their experiences. As they revisit the death over time, it will have new meaning to them.

The following are three things to remember about the way grief proceeds for children and adults:

1. *Grief proceeds on its own terms.* Chapter 7 describes the quality of grief *changing* over time; however, there is no set timeline for grief. It should not be expected for the bereaved to be "over it" after 6 months or a year or any other particular period.

2. *Grief affects many different domains in life.* It influences feelings; thoughts; behaviors; and relationships at home, work, school, and various social settings. The ways children might show the effects in school, perhaps being distractible and finding it difficult to concentrate, are discussed in Chapters 4 and 5. They are likely to have similar thoughts and experiences in other pursuits as well, such as sports, clubs, community service work, or activities related to their faith community.

3. *The expression of grief is personal and subjective.* No two people react in the same way to the death of a family member or friend.

PROVIDING STUDENTS
WITH SUPPORT OVER TIME

Feelings of loss are re-experienced in many ways as children grow, mature, and gain new insights. Children commonly have these experiences during the following:

- *Holidays.* Family holidays are not the same after a family member dies. Children miss the familiarity of their loved one's presence.

- *Transitions to a new grade or school.* The absence of a classmate or family member can be powerful at these times.

- *Special events, awards, and graduations.* Celebratory events, especially when they involve families coming together, can heighten awareness of the absence of a family member or friend.

- *Rites of passage.* As children and teens grow toward adulthood, they take a number of important steps toward maturity—first bicycle, first out-of-town trip on their own, first date, first job, first prom, first car, high school graduation. These rites are different from one family or peer group to another, but the inability to turn to the family member or friend for support, to experience their sense of pride, or to share the excitement or satisfaction often brings up feelings of grief.

Experiences involving revisiting grief may be fairly straightforward for children—something they recognize and cope with well. These experiences might also be difficult, however, because they are frightening and unexpected. They are also frustrating because it makes children feel out of control, and they can be distressing because the feelings are unpleasant and uncomfortable. Children may have feelings of shame or anxiety when these signs of grief arise.

It is helpful for bereaved children to understand the effects of grief over time and to determine how they can receive support for these feelings as they arise. Teachers can offer guidance that helps children expect a range of feelings at different times.

RESPONDING TO GRIEF TRIGGERS

Triggers of grief are common in bereavement. Grief might be triggered by anniversaries or other important events. The family holidays, the deceased's birthday, the start of a new school year, or a father–daughter dance, for example, might bring up sudden and powerful feelings of sadness. Everyday occurrences can also act as triggers—walking by a familiar corner or seeing a television show the deceased person used to enjoy.

A wide range of events can act as grief triggers in school settings. A student might come across a photo of a place the family visited on vacation a year ago. In music class, students might sing one of the deceased's favorite songs. A health class might discuss a new medicine that helps people survive the very disease that caused the death of their friend. A student might make a cruel or thoughtless joke about death. A new set of math problems might remind a student of how much she misses the help her father used to give her with her math homework.

In addition, grief triggers often catch people off guard. They can be troubling to children who are trying to keep their school day on track while trying not to think about the person who died. The emotional responses can be mild and brief. A student might have a resurgence of sadness and a few moments of distraction, and then be able to focus again. Such emotions can also be powerful and deep, bringing on sudden tears or sobs and evoking overwhelming feelings of emptiness.

Teachers who observe emotional responses to grief triggers can help students find a safe place to experience their feelings and recover their composure. This might be the office of the school counselor or school nurse, if they are available. There might be a safe place for students to step out of the classroom for a brief time—a hallway, the library, the bathroom, or the main office.

It is important that the student have a chance to talk with someone about this experience. Teachers can invite students to talk with them for a few moments after class, and they should be sure to do so if a counselor, nurse, or other support person is not available. Occasionally, a student may want to call a parent. Students should understand that these responses are natural and may continue to occur. For most people, they occur less frequently over time, although they may continue to be powerful.

Common Grief Triggers

The following are common triggers for grief that children may experience:

- Listening to a song
- Hearing a piece of information on the news
- Certain smells and sounds
- Special occasions (e.g., birthdays, holidays, Mother's and Father's Day, graduations)
- Lost opportunities (e.g., recitals, sporting activities, father–daughter dance, prom)

Helpful Responses When a Child Experiences a Grief Trigger

The following are some options for offering support if a child experiences grief triggers:

- Choose an adult or location as a safe space the child can go to if strong feelings of grief arise.
- Establish procedures to allow the child to leave the classroom with prior permission if he or she is feeling overwhelmed. This can make it more likely that the child will seek needed support.
- Let the child call a parent or family member if needed.
- Provide permission and encouragement to see the school nurse or a counselor to talk.
- Offer private teacher time to discuss feelings, concerns, or other matters.

(For more detailed suggestions, see Chapter 5.)

ONGOING SUPPORT FOR STUDENTS AND FAMILIES

Teachers can take a number of steps that offer support to grieving students and their families over time. Although these are not likely to be as intensive as the kind of assistance teachers offer immediately after a death, they can play an important role in guiding students along in the process. Students and families continue to be affected by grief, and they will appreciate the sensitivity of a teacher who offers ongoing support about their loss.

The following are some suggestions that students and families have found helpful:

- *Help preserve memories.* Children sometimes worry that they will forget the person who died, especially if they were quite young at the time of the death. Stories, pictures, and continued mention of the person who died can help children sustain their memory of the deceased. This reinforces their sense of having known and been known by this person.

  Teachers who know students who have coped with a death at some point in the past can invite them to write, talk, or draw pictures about the person. This lets students know that the teacher is supportive and concerned, as well as available to talk about these matters if they wish.

  Students may want to share some of their stories with the teacher or the class. It is important that this be a matter of choice. Some will want to share information about their family member or friend who died, and others will not.

- *Affirm the importance of strong feelings.* This is something teachers can do directly with bereaved students or in a general way with all students. Children and adolescents can benefit from opportunities to learn how to identify, describe, and cope with emotions. They can learn that strong feelings are something everyone experiences. Students might identify people who can give them support when they have strong emotions. They could develop lists of ways to cope with feelings, such as taking deep breaths, talking to a friend, talking to an adult, playing with a pet, and so forth.

  It is helpful for bereaved children to understand that their feelings are a sign of how important the person was to them. When this understanding is paired with skills for coping with strong feelings, children are less likely to be distressed by powerful emotions that arise as part of ongoing grief.

- *Maintain or increase contact with the family.* As mentioned previously, it is important for schools and teachers to make contact with families after a death occurs (see Chapter 6). Families and teachers together can assess how children are coping and plan accommodations in schoolwork if necessary, as well as other means of support. These sorts of contacts continue to be helpful over time. If there are concerns about a student's behavior, early attention can prevent problems from starting or make it possible to resolve them more quickly if they do develop.

  Some time after a death has occurred, if teachers notice grief reactions that seem especially strong, it is a good idea to check with the family. Difficulties may also be showing up in other areas.

- *Support contact between the family and the child's health care provider.* As mentioned, after a death has occurred, children often worry about their own health and that of others in their family. They are also experiencing greater stress than usual, which can cause a range of physical symptoms, including headaches and stomachaches.

  Teachers may have opportunities to encourage families to make contact with their children's pediatrician or other health care provider. These providers can help identify complaints that stem from physical illness, emotional distress, or a combination of the two. Health care providers can also direct families to community resources that support families experiencing grief, such as bereavement support groups, community mental health programs, or camps for children who have experienced the death of a family member. A health care provider may offer to talk with children to see what they understand about these events. Sometimes he or she can help children express concerns that they are not discussing with the family.

- *Remember and recognize anniversaries.* Families remember the anniversaries of a loved one's death, and the school community remembers the anniversaries of the death of a student or staff member. Children will be aware of the anniversary. Typically, they will find themselves thinking of their family member or friend more often, and more intensely, around this time.

  This can be a confusing and lonely experience. Even when students had strong support from friends and community at the time of the death of a family member, people outside the family are less likely to remember anniversaries of the death. A year later, friends have often moved on to other concerns. Schools may be reluctant to acknowledge the anniversaries of the death of a member of the school community. This can prompt children and staff to think that they are alone in experiencing distress at this time. In addition, special support, such as counseling or bereavement groups, may have ended. At this time, when their sense of support has diminished, students may find their feelings of sadness increasing. At each subsequent anniversary, children are likely to experience these same feelings of remembrance and sadness.

  Teachers can reach out to students around the time of the anniversary of the death. For example, if a student lost a parent in sixth grade, it would mean a great deal to him or her to receive a card from the teacher the following year in seventh grade. The card can acknowledge that this is probably a difficult time for the student and that the teacher is thinking of him or her.

  Similarly, one of the student's seventh-grade teachers might mention privately to the student that he or she had heard from last year's teacher about the death and knew that the anniversary was coming up. An expression of caring and condolence is very powerful and important.

  Schools can provide opportunities to acknowledge the anniversaries of deaths of students and school staff. Chapter 11 addresses the important topic of memorialization and commemoration in schools. Sometimes people worry that an acknowledgement of the anniversary will serve as a painful reminder to children. Teachers do not need to be concerned about this. Children are already thinking about the anniversary. A genuine gesture of support will be appreciated.

APPROACH TOPICS WITH
SENSITIVITY IN THE CLASSROOM AND AT SCHOOL

Because we have such extensive knowledge of world events, we hear constantly about tragedies and deaths around the world. These topics make their way into classrooms regularly through literature, history, health, current events, and other subjects. Knowing that many students have lost a family member or friend, it is important to approach such subjects with sensitivity. It is understandable that some students will find these topics distressing. Often, teachers will not know the specific students in their classes who have experienced losses. It would be difficult to anticipate what content or activities might be upsetting to individual students because teachers cannot know the full history of every student.

What Teachers Can Do

Teachers can take some simple steps when they introduce classroom activities or subjects that might be difficult for children who have experienced the death of a family member or friend. Being proactive in this way offers reassurance to all students, while also providing support and understanding to those who have experienced losses. It also models for children how to be empathic and supportive of the needs of others.

The following sections offer some suggestions for maintaining sensitivity in the classroom for children who have experienced the death of a loved one.

Providing Activities that Focus on a Loved One

In elementary school, students often prepare cards, letters, gifts, or drawings for family members. They might make cards for Mother's Day, Father's Day, Valentine's Day, or other holidays. In any given class, there is a reasonable chance that one or more students has lost a parent. In addition, there may be students who have parents who are divorced or who have parents of the same gender. Others may live with grandparents or other relatives.

Teachers can approach these activities by asking students to think about an adult who has helped raise them or has supported them in an important way. This discussion can lead naturally into a conversation about the ways we recognize and appreciate people who have helped us grow up and stay healthy and safe. Mother's Day and Father's Day are ways to acknowledge these people.

Students can then be invited to make a Mother's Day card for their mother or a card for someone else who has been an important support in their lives. A teacher might acknowledge that students have many different kinds of families, and some of them live with their mothers, whereas others do not.

A Mother's Day Card

Jack's mother died in March. In early May, his third-grade teacher handed students pieces of colorful paper and asked them to make their mothers cards for Mother's Day. Jack froze in his seat, staring straight ahead. The bright paper sat untouched on his desk. He had no idea what to do. Other students in the class knew Jack's mother had died. As they bent to their tasks, they stole glances at him, wondering what he was thinking and how he could possibly do this assignment.

His teacher walked around the classroom, checking on the students' work. When she got to Jack's desk, she saw the blank piece of paper. She said, "Jack, you can just make a card for your aunt or something." She walked on. Every student in the class watched as he slowly picked up a single crayon and began to mark listlessly on the paper in front of him.

When teachers know students who have lost a parent, they can approach them privately before these activities. Students and teachers can work out an approach to the activity that is positive for the student. For example, in the Mother's Day card activity, the teacher might say something like this:

Later today, we're going to do an activity that talks about Mother's Day, and I'm going to ask the class to make cards. Your situation is different from many of the other students in the class because your mother died earlier this year. I wanted to talk to you beforehand so we could figure out if you'd like to do this activity or if you'd rather do something else.

The point of this activity is for all of the students in the class to think about someone who has been important to them—maybe their mothers, maybe someone else—and express appreciation to that person. You can make a card or drawing about your mother if you wish, or you can make a card for someone else who cares for you. You don't need to share your work—I won't call on you— but if you want *to share, you can volunteer. Also, if you'd rather, we can come up with a different activity for you to do that doesn't focus on Mother's Day."*

These simple words let the student know that the teacher is aware of the situation, sensitive to feelings that might come up during the activity, and willing to be quite flexible about what sort of activity would be most useful.

Discussing Topics Involving Death

Characters die in novels. Current events often involve upheaval, tragedy, and death. History and social studies classes discuss wars and violence. What effects do topics such as these have on bereaved students?

Topics involving death can be difficult for students who have lost a family member or friend. This is even more likely when there is some similarity between the discussion topic and the actual death. For example, a lesson about the Vietnam War might be difficult for a student who lost a family member in the war in Afghanistan or Iraq. A novel that includes characters that are killed in a car crash would probably be challenging for a student whose friends died this way.

One of the best ways to offer support for bereaved students—both those who might be known to a teacher and those who are not identified—is to prepare all students ahead of time for the material. Before beginning the study of a novel where a death occurs, a teacher might say, "Without giving away the plot, I do want to let you know that one of the important characters in this book dies in a car crash. Some of you have probably known people who have died, perhaps in a similar way. When we read about events like this, it sometimes brings up strong emotions. If any of you have thoughts or feelings about the book that you'd like to discuss privately, please let me know. I'll arrange a time when we can talk."

Similarly, teachers can acknowledge that students might have a range of emotional responses as they address current events or discuss history. For example, a teacher might say, "We're about to see some film and photographs about the liberation of the concentration camps at the end of World War II. I want you to know that the images are disturbing. I've seen them several times and still find them upsetting. If you find yourself having strong emotional reactions, I want you to remember several things. First, it's common to have such responses. Second, it's important to talk to someone you trust about your responses. And, third, if you want to talk privately about any of your thoughts or feelings after seeing these things, let me know. I'd be happy to set up a time to talk with you."

It would also be a good idea for teachers to make a general statement at the beginning of a course that covers such events. Again, teachers can acknowledge that students might have a range of reactions to the material throughout the course.

A teacher could say, "Many of these subjects can be disturbing. Sometimes they are especially troubling for people who have had similar experiences in their own lives. For example, if your family had to leave an area where there was war or violence, it may be hard to hear about similar situations in other parts of the world. If someone you care about was wounded or killed in combat, it may be difficult to learn about wars. If you do have any strong reactions about the things we're learning in this class or worry that you might, please let me know. I'm happy to talk with you privately, or as a class, at any time about these things."

Teaching About Important National Events

In recent years, the United States has experienced a number of major events of national importance—events that have transformed us as a nation. These include the terrorist attacks of September 11, the wars in Afghanistan and Iraq, and the terrible consequences of Hurricane Katrina. Other events in the future will play an important role in our identity and history, and many of these will involve tragedy and death.

It is important for students to learn about these events as a way to understand more about themselves, their communities, and their country. At some point, the position of these events shifts in our consciousness. They are no longer what is currently happening, and they become a part of our history. When do teachers stop teaching about September 11 as a current, critical matter and begin to address it as a matter of recent American history, for example?

One of the reasons this question is difficult is that the answer is different if your own family was affected by an event. September 11, 2001, may seem like a long time ago if you are teaching students who were very young or not yet born when it occurred. However, if your class includes a student who lost an uncle in the attacks, or a parent who was in the Pentagon in Virginia or one of New York City's Twin Towers at the time, the event is still affecting the family deeply.

Recent history feels more real to everyone, including students. This means it can be more troubling. Because we live in a country where people are mobile and move often, any classroom might include students who have been personally touched by such events.

Teachers do not need to avoid teaching about these events, but it is important to be sensitive about them. They continue to touch real people across the nation, and this may well include students in their classroom. Using the principles described in the previous section, teachers can give students advance notice that difficult topics will be covered. They can mention these more current events specifically. They might survey students in a general sense about their experiences (without asking for public disclosures of personal losses) before delving deeply into content. For example, a teacher could ask, "How many of you have heard about Hurricane Katrina? Were any of you affected by the storm, or did you know people who were?" It is always important to acknowledge that students may have emotional responses to some of this material and that they can talk to the teacher about their thoughts or feelings at any time.

A Special Exhibit

A museum in one city focused on important social events in the nation's history. They had an excellent exhibit on the history of civil rights, for example. The museum had a lively educational component and was a popular destination for school field trips. Students of all ages found the exhibits interesting and informative.

A few years after the attacks of September 11, the museum planned a special temporary exhibit about the event to open on the anniversary of the attack. It included photos of the plane crashing into the second tower, the devastation on the ground, and survivors running away from the buildings. There were photographs of surviving New York firefighters and police officers next to their comments about their comrades who had died in the rescue efforts. Images showed the damage to the Pentagon and the crash site of Flight 93 in Pennsylvania.

The temporary exhibit was located immediately beyond the main entrance. All of the students on field trips who were planning to learn about the material covered in the museum's permanent exhibits would have to first walk into this room full of powerful, frightening, and recent images. There was no advance warning before walking into the exhibit. The students would have no preparation beforehand. Teachers would not be expecting the exhibit and would not know to prepare students or their families.

Coming upon these images might have been painful for any American. They could be disturbing to children just by the nature of the event and the power of the images, but it would be especially difficult for children who had been close to the event in some way. Some of the children may have had parents who worked in or near the Twin Towers or the Pentagon, some may have lost family members, some may have had friends whose parents were close to the event, and others may have simply seen a great deal of media coverage in the days and weeks after the attacks.

A museum member raised concerns about these issues, and the museum staff responded immediately. They asked the NCSCB for advice, and, working together, a plan for the exhibit was quickly developed. The museum sent out information to teachers who were planning field trips to the museum. They developed teaching materials about the exhibit for students of all ages and made these available to teachers. When classes of students arrived at the entrance, they were greeted by docents who talked about the exhibits they would see in the museum, including the special exhibit on the September 11 attacks. Museum staff and docents were also given guidelines for talking to children and adults about the exhibit. The museum made sure that the exhibit was well-staffed, especially during field trip hours.

Normalizing the Experience of Grief

Schools can also take steps to normalize the experience of grief. They can include information and lessons about death and grieving in regular coursework. They can respond to deaths that have an impact on individual students and the school community as they occur. They might also offer grief support groups in the school setting. Such groups could take a number of different forms. For example, a local hospice program might facilitate a grief group that meets weekly for 8 weeks and is open to any student who has experienced the death of a family member or friend. A school's mental health specialist might host a monthly "Remembrance" group in which students can drop in and talk about friends or family members who have died. The school's counseling services might do specific outreach to students they know who have experienced a loss of a family member or friend, as well as set up a support group for them.

SUPPORTING STUDENTS IN LIFE TRANSITIONS

Life transitions can be challenging times for bereaved students. The loss of a parent can be particularly difficult for children as they move forward in their lives and miss the special guidance and support a parent can give. Even if a death occurred many years earlier, transitions can be difficult. The following sections describe some of these challenging times, and Chapter 7 further describes some of the challenges.

Puberty

Puberty can be a very challenging time for students who have lost a loved one. The loss of a same-gender parent can be particularly troublesome at this time. Puberty can be more difficult for girls without a mother or boys without a father.

Girls who have lost their mothers may not have a comfortable source to turn to for information about how to manage menstrual periods and the physical and emotional issues that often accompany them. Tampons or pads? What do I do about cramps? Why do I feel so sad all of a sudden? What do I say to my teacher if I have to leave class because my period just started? What if my friends tease me about having my period?

Boys who have lost their fathers may be confused or frightened by wet dreams; have no clue about how to cope with unwanted erections at school; and struggle with how to respond to teasing, dares, or derogatory comments by peers. What do I do about this changing body? Why do I have these new feelings and urges? What does it mean to be a man?

In classes that discuss puberty and growing up, children are often given assignments that require talking to a parent. In classes about sexuality, students are often told, "If you have more questions about this, you can ask your parents." In a health class that is learning about friends and dating, students might be asked to talk to a parent about things they did with friends when they were young. Although every student should have a parent or guardian, these topics may be difficult to discuss with an opposite gender parent or a guardian the child does not know as well.

Teachers can be sensitive to the fact that some students do not have parents who can help them with these assignments. They may have students who had a parent who died. Or, some students may have a living parent who is unavailable for any number of reasons—deployed in the military, in prison, mentally ill, divorced, or living out of state.

This is why it is always a good idea to offer students the option of talking to their parent or another adult they know and trust, such as another family member, a coach, or a counselor. Teachers can offer to talk to students and help them identify such a support if they are having difficulty identifying someone for this role.

Dating and Relationships

As children and adolescents mature, they are likely to have crushes and become involved in romantic relationships. Many preteens and teens turn to parents for direct advice at these times. They are also looking at their parents' relationship indirectly—it serves as a model for the ways a couple communicates, negotiates differences, demonstrates caring and love, offers support to one another, and builds increasing intimacy.

If a surviving parent is not in a new relationship, is dating casually, or has had a series of partners, adolescents may miss the modeling of a steady relationship. If the surviving parent has established a new and ongoing relationship, the imperfections of the new partner may seem quite stark to a child who has naturally idealized a deceased parent. This can leave some adolescents feeling frustrated, isolated, and confused. They may engage in riskier types of relationships[1] or simply feel adrift as they try to make their way through these new kinds of relationships.

Many children are raised in single-parent households and may miss a divorced parent in similar ways. For a child whose parent has died, however, the feelings are linked to the deeper experiences of bereavement and the recognition that this person who was so important will never be able to offer support and guidance in these matters.

Transition to College

Teachers of older students who have lost a parent may be able to offer support as they near the end of high school. Students must decide whether their next steps will occur close to their family or farther away. As mentioned in Chapter 7, the best answer will be different for different students. It would be helpful for bereaved students to be offered support from a trusted teacher. A teacher might say, "I know this can be a difficult time for anyone. This is the age where you need to decide whether to stay nearby or go somewhere else after high school. Sometimes, though, this decision is especially hard for students who have lost a parent, even if the death happened some time ago. If you ever want to talk about this, I'd be happy to listen."

Bereavement and Transitions

The following are examples of issues that may come up for bereaved students, especially those who have lost a parent or family member, during school or other life transitions:

- Feeling less secure in the face of an exciting but also frightening change
- Less confidence due to loss of a parent who promoted more independence
- Loss of advice about coursework, college decisions, or future plans
- Worries about increased personal independence and separation from family when a surviving parent is still struggling to cope
- Concerns about choices that will place more financial burdens on the family (e.g., extracurricular activities, college preparatory courses, private or out-of-state colleges)
- Sense of abandoning younger siblings through increased independence or a transition to career or college
- Passing on the role as acting head of household to a younger sibling who is unprepared or struggling with bereavement issues
- Missing support in career decisions (e.g., an adolescent may have wanted to pursue the same career as the family member who died, but no longer has the person's guidance and mentorship)
- Loss of a trusted resource for support in making important life decisions

BEREAVEMENT CAN LAST A LIFETIME

At each new stage in their lives, children develop new skills for thinking and relating to others. Bereaved children will use these skills to reach a deeper and more satisfying explanation of a death. In many ways, the work of making meaning from a death never really ends; however, over time, this work becomes less difficult and takes less energy. It may start as a full-time job. Later, it becomes more of a part-time effort that allows other meaningful work and experiences to occur.

Teachers who remain sensitive to the needs and experiences of bereaved children over time can offer ongoing support that helps students make sense of these experiences and maintain a positive, productive course in their lives. One of the most important principles we promote at NCSCB is the recognition that grieving can last a lifetime, but it should not consume a life.

ENDNOTE

1.   See Adams and Deveau (1987).

9

When an Entire
School Is Affected

The death of a member of the school community—a student, teacher, or other staff member—can have a profound impact on the entire school. Teachers and other staff will have extra responsibilities to provide students with information and support and to monitor their reactions and adjustment. Often, virtually everyone will experience some sort of emotional response to the death. This can sometimes involve strong feelings of grief among many or all students and staff.

This chapter discusses some of the elements that help schools notify and provide support to students after a schoolwide loss. Although every school should have a crisis response team that has planned ahead for such events, it is also helpful for all teachers to know more about what may happen and how they can support students.

GOALS OF SUPPORT

It is important for schools to set up a system for offering students *and* staff support. This includes having school staff and/or consultants who have experience and skills in providing support after a school crisis and who are available to talk with staff and students in both group and individual settings.

The goals of support for students include the following:

- *Normalize common experiences of grief.* Anticipatory guidance helps students understand what to expect. They can hear about the range of feelings that are common in these circumstances, the ways people might express their feelings, and the ways people's feelings may change in the short and long term (i.e., the coming days, weeks, and months).

- *Help students express and cope with feelings.* Following a death, talking with students directly helps to understand what happened and to identify their feelings. They need a safe, nonjudgmental environment in which to express their reactions. In groups, they can learn coping strategies and share their own ideas. These interventions keep more students present in school at these difficult times and decrease the negative effects on learning that often accompany grief.

- *Help students find resources and strategies for coping with difficult feelings.* Many students will experience straightforward reactions to the death that are clearly expressed and match the situation well. Some, however, will have more complicated reactions. They may struggle with feelings of regret or remorse, especially if they believe they mistreated the individual at some point in the past. Others may have a sense of survivor guilt—"Why should he have been the one to drown when we've all gone swimming out at the quarry?" They may feel anxious, fearful, or angry. As previously mentioned, depressed students may experience a worsening of symptoms. Students may also feel despair or have thoughts of suicide.

  Talking with a mental health professional with expertise in bereavement or crisis can help students with troublesome feelings find productive ways to express and cope with them. They can also find resources for ongoing support if the difficult feelings seem dangerous in any way (e.g., thoughts of suicide) or do not resolve within a reasonable period of time.

- *Clarify concepts for younger students.* Younger students may have more difficulty understanding death. They are more likely to misinterpret explanations about death.

The goals for staff support are similar. School mental health professionals and qualified consultants may be helpful in providing information and support to staff. They can facilitate discussions about how teachers feel being the bearers of this information, ask about their interactions with students, and offer guidance for any situations with students or parents that they are finding difficult or confusing. Teachers can take important steps to care for themselves personally at these times, which are discussed in depth in Chapter 12.

MAJOR CRISES AND COMPLEX SITUATIONS

Some types of deaths that may touch a school community are especially complicated. They might involve major crises, such as a natural disaster, an industrial accident, a violent incident in the school or community, or an act of aggression or terrorism that directly affects the local community. Providing support to students after such events involves many of the same principles that are described throughout this book, as well as other important steps.

Planning for and responding to such major events is not the focus of this chapter or the book, but it is vitally important for schools. For those interested in learning more about how to develop school crisis preparedness and response plans, as well as how to train school crisis teams, we recommend the handbook developed by members of the NCSCB.[1]

School Crisis Plans: Responding to a Death

Schools should have a school crisis team in place that has developed a response plan in the event of a death in the school community.[2] The plan should cover how notification of a death is handled, and it should address such matters as who is notified, how people are reached, and what is said. Typically, this includes the following steps:

- *Notify and activate the school crisis team.*

- *Verify the information.* Check with the family, local authorities (e.g., the police or coroner), or other authoritative sources.

- *Determine what information is to be disclosed.* The family may express wishes on this matter. Find out what information has been publicly released through the press or local authorities.

- *Notify teachers and other staff.* An emergency meeting is often scheduled before classes begin. Teachers are informed of the death and given guidelines for notifying students and offering support.

- *Notify students.* Face-to-face notification by familiar staff in small, naturally occurring group settings is recommended. Homeroom or another class (depending on when the school learns of the death) is often a good option. It is best to avoid delivering such information in large assemblies or over the public address system. Students should all hear the same information (e.g., from a prepared, written statement). They should also be given information about support resources and offered opportunities to talk about their responses to the news. This might occur within a class discussion and by referral to a support room where mental health professionals are available. Options should be made available as soon as students hear the announcement.

- *Notify parents.* Often, this is done by a letter that is sent home with students, e-mailed, or posted on the school's web site. This letter should describe the types of support being offered to students and families.

- *Notify other schools as appropriate.* This might include feeder schools, where the deceased was known by teachers or younger students, or schools attended by siblings of the deceased. In smaller communities, it may be appropriate to notify all schools.

Following these steps gives schools a better opportunity to ensure that students learn of the death in an appropriate setting—that is, with a familiar teacher who has been prepared and is ready to make the announcement. Students can then be connected to support services more easily and effectively.

A Pity About Mr. Sutton

Maddy was walking down the hallway at her high school early one Monday morning before many students had arrived. Her band teacher, Mr. Thompson, walked by reading a memo. She greeted him.

"Hello, Maddy!" he said brightly. "How was your weekend?" Then he pointed to his memo. "Wow. What a pity about Mr. Sutton."

Mr. Sutton was the school's French teacher. He was a prickly, troublesome character as far as many of the teachers were concerned and not well-known except by students taking French. Many of those students found him difficult—a teacher with high standards and an unforgiving attitude about late assignments or poor test scores. However, he had a small and devoted following of advanced students who performed well in his classes, enjoyed his unique brand of irony, and blossomed under his focused and carefully planned lessons. Maddy was one of those students.

"What happened?" she asked, thinking he must have broken a leg, had his car stolen, or lost his dog.

"He died of a heart attack Saturday night. And he was only 38. What a shock."

"He…what?" said Maddy, confused. She reached out and took the memo from Mr. Thompson's hand. She squinted at the words and tried to make sense of them. "There must be a mistake," she said, growing ashen. "Is this a joke? This can't be real. He…he was fine on Friday. He has two kids. What did you say happened?"

Mr. Thompson look startled. "I'm sorry. I didn't realize you knew him," he said, looking and feeling awkward. "Well, I've got to get on to my class," he said rather abruptly, taking back the memo and walking away. "How was I to know?" he thought to himself. "She never said she was taking French."

Maddy stood alone in the hallway, tears brimming in her eyes. She had never known anyone who had died before. She turned around slowly, making a full circle. She saw no one she knew.

When schools have well-designed, up-to-date crisis plans in place, teachers will be better prepared to speak with students about a school death. They will know what resources for support are available. They will understand that students may have powerful emotional responses, and they will direct them when appropriate to counselors who can listen to their reactions and guide them through the process.

Making Sure All Students Are Informed

Another important consideration is making sure that all students have been informed about the death. On any given day, some students will not be at school. They may be out sick, away on a field trip for the day, or on a longer class trip to science camp or a music festival. How will students in each of these situations hear the information?

It is difficult for students to come back to a school community that has experienced something this profound when they do not feel included. This can lead to anxiety, misunderstandings, and a sense of isolation.

Although each situation is different, the following are some possible solutions:

- Schools might call or send e-mails to the parents of students who are not in school that day to provide the necessary information, as well as suggestions about talking with their children.

- A school administrator might plan to meet a class returning from a field trip to share the news with them. A call to the teacher's cell phone before they return will allow him or her to make sure students stay together on their return so they can hear the announcement and receive support.

- Teachers at camps or festivals that involve overnight trips could be contacted by the school. Copies of the announcement about the death, as well as supportive material for student discussions, could be e-mailed or faxed to teachers in most settings. It is usually best to share this news with students promptly. Many are likely to be checking in with families and friends and will hear some of the information from them. Students who learn of the news at school will often communicate quickly by text messages or via cell phone. This can leave students in the difficult position of informing others who have not yet heard the news (e.g., friends, classmates, teachers). This is an unfair burden for students.

- During summer vacation or over a holiday period, news of a death may appear in local papers or other news outlets. The school might choose to contact students' families by e-mail or telephone trees to relay the information. In some situations, especially if the death is likely to have a significant impact on many students, the school may decide to open for a day or an evening. Students and families could be invited to come in to talk with counselors if they wish.

- After a summer or holiday period, announcements should be given in all classes so that students who might have missed the information during the break are appropriately informed.

Shared Experiences of Grief

What happens in a school when so many people are sharing an experience of grief? The following are some common occurrences among students:

- *Everything is multiplied.* When one grieving student looks around, he or she sees other grieving students. One person crying might start several other people crying. One anxious student might heighten anxiety in three other students. One act of compassion inspires others. Both positive and negative coping behaviors are likely to be repeated and multiplied many times.

- *Anxiety can grow.* It was previously mentioned that death challenges our *assumptions* about the things that will stay in place in our world (see Chapter 7). We can no longer feel assured that our family members will be waiting for us at home in the evening. When many students in a school are experiencing this effect, anxiety may become higher for all students.

- *Students come with a range of experience and understanding.* Although bereavement is a common experience among children, many students may have never experienced the death of someone they personally know well. They will be having these experiences of grief, anxiety, and confusion for the first time. Other students are likely to have already experienced a death. They will have some basic understandings about grief—they know it is intense, it is confusing, and that it may persist for awhile, but it does not throw you off track forever.

- *Information spreads quickly.* Death is compelling and raises anxiety for almost everyone. People naturally want to know about these events. Staff and students will talk among themselves about what happened. This creates a ripe environment for passing along information as well as for spreading rumors.

This is one reason it is so important to inform the entire school of a death at the same time—it gives all students the same level of knowledge. Otherwise, some students will hear an accurate statement provided by their teachers, and other students will pick up rumors or bits of overheard conversation. When information is inaccurate or incomplete, anxiety and complicated reactions are more likely.

• *Students are confused about what is expected.* Children and teens who have not experienced grief at a group level, or who have never gone through something this serious, may feel uncertain about what to do and how to behave. Particularly among adolescents, who sometimes have an "imaginary audience" in their minds, there may be some rumination about what is expected. "Did I cry enough? Or was that too much?" "Am I supposed to look really serious and sad even if I don't feel that way?" "Am I supposed to act like I'm actually reading this assignment in class today, when I can't concentrate on anything?"

• *Some students will naturally be more empathic.* Some students seem to know what to say or do to help themselves, peers, and even teachers feel better. These students can provide positive role modeling and emotional support for their classmates. This is one of the benefits of having students share experiences and ideas about how to deal with grief. They can reach out to one another, offer support, and learn from each other. However, it is important to recognize that a student who appears to be handling the situation well may also benefit from support. These students should not be expected to carry extra burdens as the school community copes with the loss.

• *Teachers can have a range of powerful reactions.* All of these experiences can be compounded by the fact that teachers and other staff are also having powerful reactions. Teachers may have many of the same responses students do—difficulty concentrating, uncertainty about how to act and what to say, confusion, anxiety, and a sense of being overwhelmed by the concentration of grief in the school community.

Often, a few teachers have had a special connection with a student who has died. They may have offered tutoring and mentorship to the student, encouraged extra plans or projects, sponsored the student in competitions, or had other opportunities to build a stronger-than-usual relationship. Some teachers step into roles almost as surrogate parents. They may be personally devastated by the death of a student they admired and cared about.

When an announcement about a death is made schoolwide, teachers may also find themselves experiencing something quite different from their students. If a sixth-grade student dies, for example, the second-grade students may not have known him or her, but their teacher who makes the announcement to the class may have taught this student. Similarly, if a teacher or school administrator dies, students may not have known the person well and may have a mild response to news of the death. Their teacher, however, may be feeling grief related to the loss of a colleague or friend, along with a sense of personal vulnerability (i.e., "Could such a death happen to me?").

GIVING SUPPORT TO STUDENTS

As discussed previously, teachers can make a meaningful difference in times of grief by establishing an authentic and supportive connection with students. The following are some steps that will be especially useful when a school is reacting to a death in their community.[3] Most of these will sound familiar because they are similar to the steps recommended for individual students experiencing grief.

- *Know the guidelines of the school for these situations.* Schools should make guidelines available to teachers through an Intranet site or written documents, or in other ways. Every teacher should have access to copies of crisis plans at any time. Familiarity with the plan should be developed through ongoing training and exercises. If the school does not have crisis plans in place, teachers should advocate for their development.

- *Remember that any student may be deeply affected.* It is impossible to know the experiences of every student. Any student may be deeply affected by a death, so it is important that teachers speak sensitively about the incident to all students.

- *Be approachable.* Teachers who can talk about complex and difficult topics, including death and grief, are more likely to be approached by students looking for support. Teachers should take opportunities to discuss these matters in an open, authentic manner; for example, by talking with a class about common grief reactions or by discussing how receiving support for troublesome feelings can be helpful.

- *Listen.* When students want to share, it can be especially powerful for them simply to have an attentive listener. The focus should be on them.

- *Protect students.* Teachers should take steps to protect students from being retraumatized about the death. Emotionally expressive students might be teased by others for crying. Reporters might want to talk to students about the death. A television in a common area might be tuned to a news station repeating details about the death.

- *Make connections.* The strategies described in Chapter 5 can be used to make authentic and positive connections with students. Teachers should invite them to talk about their thoughts and experiences.

- *Teach about grief and normalize receiving support.* Teachers can help students understand common reactions to grief, including having strong feelings, being confused, feeling out of control, and so forth. They can emphasize the importance of reaching out for support and the power of giving support to others. Teachers can also include suggestions about when seeking help is especially important (e.g., when troublesome feelings persist or get worse) and provide resources (e.g., the support room set up by the school after a crisis).

- *Be a positive role model.* It is okay for students to see their teachers' emotions, as well as some of the ways they are coping with their feelings. This helps them understand how to express their own feelings and come up with strategies for coping. For example, a teacher might say to her class, "I was shocked when

I heard the news, and I just felt like crying." Or, "When I heard about the car crash, I felt frightened. I was even nervous when I got in the car this morning." Then the teacher could offer an example of coping. "After I cried, I talked to my husband (or sister, friend), and it helped me feel better. Who is someone you could talk to if you were feeling sad?" Or, "I took a couple of deep breaths, made sure my seatbelt was fastened, and was very attentive the whole time I drove here."

- *Watch for signs of distress now and over time.* Teachers can use the guidelines that were reviewed in Chapter 7 to identify students showing signs of distress. They should then provide referrals when appropriate. Although a school crisis plan, including drop-in counseling support, may be in place for a week or so, powerful feelings might come up for some students for weeks, months, or even a year or more after the incident.

- *Seek personal support.* These experiences are deeply emotional for teachers. Crisis response plans should provide support for them as well. Teachers should consider visiting the staff support room or talking with one of the counselors even if they do *not* feel a strong need to do so. This provides good role modeling for students and colleagues. We also find this type of support helpful for people who are coping well with a loss, and we recommend it to teachers who have worked in a school setting that has experienced a crisis or death.

REACHING OUT TO STUDENTS AT HIGHER RISK

As mentioned in Chapter 7, some students have a higher risk for emotional distress after a school death. A well-planned crisis response plan takes the special circumstances of these students into account. For example, a member of the crisis response team might spend the day walking through the schedule of a deceased high school student to be available to talk to classmates in any of the student's classes. A mental health specialist might make individual contact with the student's best friends. One of the counselors might speak with the student's teammates on the basketball team or members of clubs the student had joined.

All students should have an opportunity to meet privately with a mental health professional if they wish. This meeting could include a check-in about the student's feelings, as well as some anticipatory guidance for other feelings that may come up in coming days, weeks, or months. It is also important for students to know where they can go if they wish to talk with someone about their feelings or to address questions in the future.

Students who have a greater risk for more complex reactions include

- *Students who were close friends of the deceased.* Students who were close to the deceased, or who felt a special connection in some way, are likely to have strong grief reactions.

- *Students who shared a class with the deceased.* Classmates of the deceased are more likely to have had close personal connections and respond more strongly to the death.

- *Students who shared extracurricular activities with the deceased.* This would include clubs, sports teams, community-based groups, faith groups, and groups in other nonschool settings.

- *Students who had a complicated or difficult relationship with the deceased.* When relationships are troubled, there is a greater likelihood of more complex reactions after the death. A student who had ended a romantic relationship with the student who died might feel guilty. Someone who just had a bitter argument with the deceased that ended with threats of violence might feel a sense of relief and then a sense of guilt. A student who had a secret crush on the person might feel unable to express grief openly, even if it is quite strong.

- *Students who shared some meaningful characteristic with the deceased.* This might be some feature that heightened the surviving student's sense of identification with the deceased (e.g., "We both drew manga comics."). Or, it might be some characteristic related to the cause of death. For example, if a student dies of a chronic disease, other students with the same disease have a greater risk of distress. If a student who has been bullied commits suicide, other students who are being bullied may be at risk for suicidal behaviors.

- *Students with a history of prior losses or emotional difficulties.* The death of a friend or classmate will often act as a trigger for grief about earlier losses or bring up feelings about past or current difficulties, such as parental separation or divorce.

- *Students who have already known someone who died from similar causes.* Having previously known someone who died of similar causes is also likely to act as a trigger for earlier grief experiences.

- *Students who may worry about similar losses.* A student whose mother is ill with cancer may become very upset when a classmate dies of cancer.

- *Students with preexisting conditions.* Students with mental health issues, such as depression or anxiety disorders, may have a more difficult time coping with their feelings after a classmate's death. Anyone who has expressed suicidal thoughts or participated in self-harming behaviors may be at particularly high risk.

SPECIAL CASES: SUICIDE AND HOMICIDE

Suicide and homicide raise special concerns for schools and students. When there has been a homicide, particularly when it is gang related, friends of the deceased may feel a need to avenge the death. This can lead to escalating cycles of violence, as well as further injury and death.

When a student dies by suicide, other students who are feeling hopeless, helpless, and isolated may find thoughts of suicide emerging. This may be especially likely if the death results in attention that feels positive to an isolated or depressed student. For example, other students at the school might say, "I feel terrible about this. I'll never forget him. I'll always regret not being a better friend." A student who feels left out and overlooked might yearn for that kind of attention as well.

It is important to talk about these deaths carefully and without glamorizing the victims in any way, but still acknowledging the grief of survivors who lost a friend and a classmate. Teachers can be proactive and set the tone for students. This would include educating students about warning signs of suicide and emphasizing that thoughts of suicide are not a normal response to grief. Schools can distribute information about hotlines and support sources. The act of seeking support can be destigmatized. Students should also be encouraged to speak to an appropriate adult if they are worried that a friend or peer is thinking about suicide.

Special Circumstances: Suicide of a Student

The suicide of a student creates unique issues for schools. Important steps for schools include the following:

1. Clarify with the family what information they wish disclosed about the death. If necessary, gently explain why frank discussion that the death may be the result of suicide may allow assistance to be provided to other students and decrease the risk of additional attempts. Try to find out if information has already been shared publicly by a reliable source (e.g., local news reports). The medical examiner's determination of cause of death can come well after the event, and in some cases it may not be clear that a suicide occurred. In discussions with students, rumors and questions about suicide can be used as an opportunity to provide information about suicide prevention without confirming the cause of death as suicide.

2. Identify students considered at greatest risk for mental health distress.

3. Educate students, staff, and parents about warning signs of suicide. Distribute information about hotlines and support services widely.

4. Encourage students to seek support. Destigmatize seeking help, and affirm the importance of communication with others who can help.

5. Explicitly tell students not to keep secrets about these matters. They cannot and should not honor a request to keep a peer's report that he or she is thinking of committing suicide a secret.

6. Avoid romanticizing or glamorizing the individual or the cause of death. Although it is appropriate to acknowledge the person who died, it is also important to avoid gestures that might make these acts seem appealing to depressed or isolated students.

7. Minimize media coverage of the suicide.

8. Be aware of any deaths by suicide in the larger community. Good communication with other area schools, community mental health agencies, and the local police make this possible.

Was It the Choking Game?

A school was notified that a 13-year-old boy at the school was accidentally strangled when the cord of his hooded jacket caught on a tree branch in his back yard. He was alone at the time this happened, and his body was discovered later.

The school crisis team informed teachers of the incident and provided a written announcement that they could read to their classes. The statement indicated that the cause of death was believed to be accidental strangulation. Teachers were told that the medical examiner was continuing to investigate the death. Teachers were also given guidelines for discussion with their students, including information about common reactions to news of a death, resources for support, and opportunities for students to make comments or ask questions.

They also let teachers know that there might be questions about the cause of death. They understood that students might find it difficult to believe that a 13-year-old died accidentally this way. Students might reasonably wonder if this was a suicide or perhaps an instance of someone playing a fainting or choking game.[4] Teachers were offered suggestions for how to answer these questions.

If someone asked, for example, "Wasn't it the choking game?" they could respond by saying, "We don't know if it was, but it sounds like you may have heard something about this issue. Let's talk about that. What do you know about the choking game?"

If a student said, "A friend of mine said that guy killed himself," the teacher could reply by saying, "We don't really know if that's the reason for John's death, but suicide is an important issue, even if it wasn't what happened here. Let's take a few minutes to address some questions or concerns you may have about suicide." The teacher could then guide the discussion to general issues about suicide. Who would students go to if they were feeling sad? What are some warning signs that mean it is important for someone to get help? Who could they talk to if they had concerns about a friend's mood or behaviors?

Teachers were also given some guidelines to help them talk about the problems with rumors and speculation and to encourage students to stick to what was known in the discussion. This approach allowed teachers to focus on the concerns and anxieties of the students, even in the face of incomplete information about the student who died. It prepared teachers realistically for the experiences they would have with students. It also allowed the school, despite some challenging circumstances, to provide appropriate intervention and support for the students after this disturbing event.

DEATH OF A PROMINENT PERSON

Sometimes someone prominent in the nation, the community, or the world of students dies. It might be a politician, an actor, or a pop music star. It might be a basketball player who dies suddenly on the court during the game, which was witnessed by hundreds or (for an NBA game) millions of fans. Death might result from a highly public event, such as the 1986 space shuttle Challenger disaster, which was witnessed by students of all ages everywhere in the country.

These incidents can be expected to create many of the same kinds of reactions as a death in the school community. Students may have heightened anxiety about their own safety and that of family members and friends. They may worry about their future. Children dealing with challenges or deaths in their own families may experience greater distractibility, anxiety, and emotionalism.

For the most part, teachers will find the same skills they have used in other situations concerning death and grief useful at these times. They should help students recognize their emotional responses and make sense of the event. What emotions are they having? What kinds of things can they do to feel better? How can they ask others for support? How can they support each other?

It is also important to protect children from further trauma about the incident. Turn off television stations that are showing the incident repeatedly or endlessly analyzing reactions. Keep the focus on positive coping. Remind students that emotional responses to such events are normal and expected.

PLANNING MAKES THE DIFFERENCE

Events that affect an entire school community will always be challenging for schools, teachers, and students. It is painful to learn about the death of someone we know, especially if it is someone we also cared for. Schools that take steps to have effective plans in place will not take away that pain. They will, however, have the greatest likelihood of giving students and staff the support and resources that will be most useful for them at these difficult times.

ENDNOTES

1. See Schonfeld, Lichtenstein, Kline, and Speese-Linehan (2002). For an earlier article that summarizes the school crisis preparedness and response model, see Schonfeld, Kline, and Members of the Crisis Intervention Committee (1994). A brief overview of the School Crisis Response Initiative (Schonfeld & Newgass, 2003) can be freely downloaded at http://www.ojp.usdoj.gov/ovc/publications/bulletins/schoolcrisis/ncj 197832.pdf

2. The NCSCB has developed practical guidelines on how schools can respond to the death of a student or staff member that can be freely downloaded from the NCSCB's web site at: http://www.cincinnatichildrens.org/svc/alpha/s/school-crisis/guidelines-bereavement.htm. These guidelines summarize some of the information already covered in this book. Sample notification letters that can be downloaded as template Word documents can also be found as part of these guidelines. See also Schonfeld (2007), which can be downloaded at http://ercm.ed.gov/views/documents/Coping W_Death_StudentOrStaff.pdf

3. A resource for psychological first aid for school teachers and students titled *Listen, Protect, and Connect—Model & Teach* (Schreiber, Gurwitch, & Wong, 2006) provides further recommendations that build on those found in this section. The document

can be freely downloaded from the Ready.Gov web site at http://www.ready.gov/kids/_downloads/PFA_SchoolCrisis.pdf. A related guidance document (Schreiber, Gurwitch, Wong, & Schonfeld, 2006) is intended for use by parents, families, and other caregivers in the setting of a natural disaster and can be freely downloaded from the NCSCB web site at http://www.cincinnatichildrens .org/assets/0/78/1067/4357/4389/9f9cb2c0-b983-42bb-8b99-aba3b8ad74e9.pdf

4. Fainting or choking games are used by children as a means to create a partial or complete loss of consciousness by hyperventilating (sometimes followed by then applying pressure to the chest) or using ligatures around the neck or other means of strangulation, which often involves the assistance of other children. This can lead to a short period of lightheadedness or feeling "high." Severe injuries, brain damage, and death are possible.

10

Seriously Ill Students

When Death Is a Concern

Recent decades have seen many advances that help children with serious medical conditions live longer, more functional lives. Schools now integrate students with disabilities and serious medical issues into general education classrooms. Shorter hospitalizations and more assistive technology allow medically fragile children to live at home and attend school. Technologies also make it possible for children with very serious illnesses to attend regular classrooms. Students at a terminal stage of illness might be in the classroom until very close to the time of death.

As a result, teachers today are more likely than ever before to have students with serious conditions in their classrooms. Children with conditions that are quite complicated are sometimes able to participate in regular classrooms or alternate between home or hospital schooling and the classroom. While in the hospital, some children may also participate using live web cams or other technologies that help them stay involved in class activities.

Teachers have unique opportunities to offer guidance and support in these circumstances in several areas. They can offer support to

- The child with a serious illness
- Other students and their families
- The family of the child with the illness
- Other teachers and school staff

It is also important for teachers working with seriously ill children to receive support for their own reactions and feelings (see Chapter 12).

Teachers often have concerns about talking to a child who is seriously ill. They may be anxious that they will not know what to say or that they will say something that makes the situation more difficult. They might worry that talking with these children about their illness will make them frightened or sad. These are understandable concerns; however, once again, many of the guidelines already described for grieving children also work in these instances. It is not desirable or realistic, for example, to take away children's sadness or to find the "right" answers to all of their questions. Rather, the goal is to listen to their concerns and accept any expression of emotions. Offering this kind of support is the best way to help children find their own coping techniques.

Teachers have a unique role in the lives of these children. As has been mentioned many times, teachers are trusted sources of information, and, therefore, children can ask them questions. A teacher's goal is to help children learn. Children can engage with teachers in ways that affirm that they are living actively, have important tasks to pursue, have something to contribute to their class, and are making plans for the future—even if it is the near future. Children do not usually feel the same obligations to protect teachers that they feel about family members. They are less concerned that their teachers cannot cope with their questions or concerns about illness, disability, or death.

All of these qualities contribute to the possibility of open and forthright communication between teachers and students who are seriously ill. This is immensely valuable to the children, and one of the greatest gifts a teacher can offer.

Terminology About Children Who Are Ill

Many different terms are used to describe the circumstances of children with serious illnesses. These are the terms used in this book. Several of these might apply to the same child.

- *Life-changing condition.* A serious medical condition that changes the day-to-day activities of a child over a long period of time. This might or might not be a condition that could be fatal. Children with life-changing conditions might need to take medications or participate in treatments, and they might have physical limitations or be unable to participate in some of the usual activities of childhood. Examples include diabetes, sickle cell disease, cancer, and severe asthma.

- *Potentially life-limiting condition.* A serious illness or medical condition that on average has the potential to significantly shorten the individual's life span, such as cystic fibrosis or Duchenne muscular dystrophy.

- *Serious illness.* An illness that poses a significant threat to a child's life or well-being. It may result in disability. It is usually chronic (ongoing), but it may develop from an acute condition as well.

- *Terminal illness.* A disease or condition that is expected to result in death. In general, this term is avoided even with very serious illnesses until death is imminent. This allows people with such conditions to focus on life and the future, just as others do, for as long as possible.

In this chapter, *serious illness* is used as a sort of umbrella term for all of these situations. When *terminal illness* is used, it is in reference to a child expected to die within a matter of weeks or months at most, which is likely at some point during the current school year.

CHILDREN WHO ARE SERIOUSLY ILL

Many medical conditions can change children's lives in profound ways. Any time children have physical limitations or chronic symptoms, need regular medications or treatments, and require regular medical monitoring of their condition, they have a life-changing condition. Some of these conditions are life threatening—children may or may not recover, and they have a risk of dying as a result of the condition. Some are chronic illnesses that can be well managed over time or result in disabilities that affect daily functioning. Some are conditions that are likely to be terminal, but the time frame is uncertain—perhaps this year, perhaps in 20 years. Some are conditions that are expected to be terminal in the short term: Children who have them are expected to die within weeks or months.

Although many of the guidelines in this chapter are useful for children with any type of life-changing medical condition, the focus is primarily on children in the following two groups:

1. Children with serious acute medical problems that are potentially life threatening. Even if these children are *likely* to be cured, there is a genuine possibility that they will not be cured and may die as a result of the condition. This would include many forms of childhood cancer.

2. Children who are expected to die within a matter of weeks or months—likely at some point during the current school year.

PHYSICAL SYMPTOMS OF CHILDREN WHO ARE SERIOUSLY ILL

Children who are seriously ill can have a wide range of symptoms. Some symptoms are mild, whereas others are quite severe. Some children may look sick, whereas others may appear as energetic and healthy as other students. Sometimes children experience more discomfort from the treatments than from the illness itself.

Some children may be diagnosed with a condition that could be life limiting, but they demonstrate only a few signs of acute illness or disability. Some will focus more on the immediate experiences of medications or illness—fatigue, stomachaches, weight loss—without being especially concerned about whether their condition will end in death. Especially for younger children, the limitations in their life in the present may be more compelling than concerns about greater limitations, or death, in the future.

Some children may have serious and potentially life-limiting conditions but may show no outward signs of them. These children may nonetheless worry privately about the possibility of their own death. When discussing the needs or concerns of one student with a serious illness in a class, remember that there may be other students who have similar issues who are not identified.

Something No One Knows

Kevin, an 8-year-old boy, became tearful when his classroom was talking about the death of a classmate's sibling, but he was otherwise silent during the discussion. Afterward, his teacher spoke to him privately and asked whether there was anything special that was troubling him.

Kevin confided that a couple of years before, he had suffered from a bleeding episode in his brain. There had been no permanent damage, but he knew that the malformation that led to the bleed was too deep in his brain to be removed safely. As a result, he was always at risk of another bleeding episode, and any bleed could cause a stroke or be fatal.

Kevin's teacher had been completely unaware of this situation. Although he had realized that some of his students might be affected by the classroom discussion in ways he had not anticipated, this experience reinforced how important it was to speak sensitively about such matters to every class.

COMMON CONCERNS OF CHILDREN WHO ARE TERMINALLY ILL

Even children who are terminally ill should be allowed, even encouraged, to continue to have hope and go on with their lives. An important goal is to help these children optimize the quality of life remaining to them.

Sometimes the most extraordinary experience children with a serious or terminal illness can have is one of normalcy. They want to feel—for a month, a week, a day, or even a few moments—just like the other children in the classroom. This means that important routines should be continued with as little disruption as possible. Because school and learning are the main work in children's lives, children who are seriously or terminally ill should be allowed to attend school when possible and continue schoolwork when they are in the hospital. Membership in clubs or groups may be able to continue. Chores in the home or the classroom are appropriate when children are physically capable of completing them.

I Want to Be in Class

Tracy, a 6-year-old girl, had a recurrent brain tumor. It was inoperable and did not respond to chemotherapy. Her condition was expected to be fatal, and as the cancer progressed, she had increasing physical problems. She lost her hair during chemotherapy. Steroid medications had caused bloating. Her eyes became crossed as the tumor increased in size. She walked with increasing difficulty.

Some of the parents were not comfortable with Tracy remaining in class. They worried that her increasing disfigurement and disability would frighten their children. Some felt she was taking too much of the teacher's attention and that other students were not getting their fair share. Several worried that her impending death would be too difficult for the class. They suggested it would be best for both the class and Tracy to continue her schooling at home.

Tracy enjoyed school and her friends, and she told her mother repeatedly, "I want to be in class." She was bright and interested in learning. She was able to continue most of her schoolwork, although she occasionally needed help with writing and was not able to walk without assistance. She liked being around the other children. Tracy's mother effectively advocated that she should be allowed to continue in school. She attended class until shortly before she died at home one weekend.

Her classmates continued to see her as their friend and an active member of the class until the time of her death. They learned to respect the contributions each person could make irrespective of health or disability. After Tracy's death, the class was proud that they stood by their friend, especially when she was most in need. They were also grateful that they had been able to learn from her and benefit from her friendship.

HOW CHILDREN WHO ARE TERMINALLY ILL UNDERSTAND DEATH

As discussed in Chapter 3, children have different levels of understanding about death. Children who are terminally ill[2] might struggle with the Four Concepts About Death just as other children do. Even if they have been told little about their medical condition, most of these children usually appreciate the seriousness of their illness and develop a precocious understanding of death.[3,4,5] They often have a sophisticated appreciation of their own mortality. They realize that their time is limited and that their situation has a powerful impact on their family and others in their lives. They may have a range of complex feelings about their circumstances, including sadness, fear, resignation, or anger.

Sometimes, families or health care providers are not forthcoming with children who are seriously or terminally ill about their health status. Understandably, they wish to protect children from distress, fear, and sadness. However, it is not helpful to mislead children in these situations. In almost every case, it is appropriate, and even kind, to inform children about their health status.

Teachers may find themselves in a difficult situation if parents have decided to mislead their child about a life-threatening condition. When a teacher is asked by parents to be dishonest or withholding in the face of a student's serious illness, a parent meeting would be appropriate. Teachers in this situation should seek the assistance of a school mental health professional or consultant. (Working with families is discussed later in this chapter.)

Once children who are terminally ill understand the basic concepts about death and realize that they are likely to die soon, some will choose to talk openly about it. Others will choose to avoid the discussion. Either course is acceptable.

Acknowledging Death Openly

Children who openly acknowledge their impending death may ask surprisingly direct questions. "What will dying feel like?" "How will you remember me?" "Who will get my bicycle?" This level of frankness sometimes makes adults uncomfortable. Parents, health care providers, friends, and neighbors may all find it difficult to speak so directly about death with children. Children are sensitive to others' discomfort, and children who are terminally ill often feel they must protect their parents or others from the sadness that their impending death causes. They may join parents in a mutual pretense that they are unaware of the seriousness of their situation. They may talk about the things they will do when they get better, just to help everyone else feel more at ease.

This conspiracy of silence has a cost for children who are terminally ill. They may become emotionally isolated from others because they cannot fully express the complex feelings they are having. They cannot utilize services designed specifically for children who are terminally ill because that would break the pretense. They cannot openly express their wishes about making the most of the time that remains to them.

Dying is a difficult, confusing, often painful, and sometimes frightening process. Children who are going through this deserve as much emotional support and honesty as possible. Teachers who can handle the direct comments and questions of a child who is terminally ill offer a powerful resource for support, especially if others have been unable to provide this.

Denying or Avoiding Death

Some children choose not to discuss their impending death directly. Once they have been clearly informed, it is rarely necessary or appropriate to confront children with the fact that they are likely to die. Instead, parents, health care providers, and teachers can offer indirect outlets for expression. For example, children might express thoughts, feelings, or questions through play, art, or writing. They might respond to a story they read, a television show or movie they watched, or a video game they played. They might get quite excited about a popular song or other piece of music that expresses some of the feelings they are having.

If teachers and other adults make these outlets available, children will use them when they are ready. They will express their thoughts and feelings directly or indirectly. They may seek different types of support from different people. All of this is good—it helps children continue to explore and examine this powerful experience in their lives, as well as work to make sense of it.

QUESTIONS AND FEELINGS

Children who are terminally ill have questions and strong feelings about their situation. Many of these are the same kinds of questions and feelings that adults who are facing death have. Often, the greatest concern is about the *process* of dying, rather than death itself. Although every child and situation is different, the following are some of the common issues that emerge for children who are terminally ill:

- *Pain.* Concerns about pain are powerful for anyone with a serious illness. Children who are terminally ill have often experienced significant pain in medical procedures or as a result of their condition. They recognize that their symptoms are worsening as their condition progresses. Their pain may increase over time. Children may also experience periods of increasing anxiety as they face upcoming medical procedures that they expect to be painful. Reassurance that pain will be managed actively and effectively, both as their illness progresses and at the time of death, is an important message from family and health care providers.

- *The future.* Some children will have questions about the future, and in particular about what the world (e.g., their family, their classroom) will be like after they have died. Other children are uncomfortable talking about the future, and they avoid mentioning a time when they will not be alive.

- *Abandonment.* Children may worry that they will be separated from family as their condition worsens. They may be concerned about hospital stays that isolate them from friends, pets, and sometimes, family members. Some children may attempt to hide symptoms or force themselves to appear more energetic so that they seem more "normal" to their families.

- *Spiritual matters.* Some children have questions about religion, spirituality, and the afterlife. This may be the case whether their family is religious or not. They may find spiritual practices and beliefs comforting. They may also ask questions about God, including how God could let this illness occur.

- *Concerns about time.* Children may become frustrated at having a sense of limited time available to them, and they may be anxious or angry about wasting time.

- *Creating distance.* Some children act in ways that create distance with others. They may be angry or withdrawn. This might also be a reaction to their fear of abandonment. They create the distance first, before someone else can leave them.

- *Control.* As an illness progresses, children who are terminally ill increasingly lose control over how they feel physically and what they are able to do. They may begin to act more controlling in other ways as this occurs.

- *Sadness.* Children feel grief about their own death and about leaving behind the people and things they love. They grieve the future they will not live to see. They feel sad about the things they can no longer do because of their illness.

- *Regression.* Some children who are terminally ill regress in their behaviors and begin acting like younger children.

- *Emotional outbursts.* Children often experience and express anger, sadness, frustration, and fear more powerfully.

- *Acts of generosity and compassion.* Children who are terminally ill may also be inspired to act in generous and compassionate ways. They may reassure a family member or friend that they are okay. They may make special gifts for people to remember them by. They may create beautiful thank-you cards for people who have given them support. They may say things that help others recognize and appreciate the preciousness of life.

Teachers might see any of these behaviors in school. In most cases, they will not be especially disruptive; however, when necessary, teachers can set limits with students who are acting inappropriately around other students. It is also important to use these opportunities to reach out to children who are terminally ill and invite them to talk about their feelings or thoughts. A sympathetic, patient listener can be a great help to children in these circumstances and can often calm troublesome behaviors. If problem behaviors persist, it would be appropriate to make a referral to school counseling services or speak with the health care team to see what kinds of psychosocial support are being offered.

GUILT AND SHAME

Children and adolescents may use magical thinking to explain the cause of their illness. They may assume that their illness is the result of some wrongdoing—that they are being punished for something they did or did not do, or even something they only thought or felt. Older children or adolescents may also hear popular theories about the causes of illness and attribute their condition to such things as dietary choices, negative attitudes, or an inability to believe in their power to heal themselves. These beliefs can cause feelings of guilt—"If I could *really* believe, I could heal myself."

Children may also feel shame about having a serious illness because it represents an extreme example of being out of control. Symptoms and responses to medication may also result in shame—vomiting, diarrhea, gas, fatigue, bloating, changes in weight, hair loss, and so forth. Children need to be reassured frequently that they are not responsible for their illness. Physical changes and symptoms can be acknowledged as unpleasant but also normalized as a typical part of the process of having the condition or going through a treatment.

SEARCH FOR MEANING

Similar to adults, children and adolescents who are terminally ill may also engage in a search for meaning. What is the purpose of their lives? What gives their lives value if they are not able to accomplish their long-term goals and dreams? What is the value of a life lived so briefly?

These are questions all of us must answer for ourselves. Children with a religious background may find assistance with their questions through spiritual concepts. For people of all ages, a life well lived often means being able to help others.

Teachers and others working with children who are terminally ill can affirm their questions about life and meaning by offering to listen. They can encourage continued thought about the issues and affirm things that the child offers to others. This could be something abstract, such as hope, inspiration, or an example of courage. It might be a personality feature, such as being able to make others laugh or think, or making a commitment to doing what is right. It might also be something concrete, such as a poem shared with others, a drawing of a favorite tree, or a thoughtful letter.

Children may also want to complete a particular activity or project. This can give them a feeling of accomplishment and the comforting sense that they have created something of enduring value that will outlive them. Teachers and classmates may find it especially gratifying to assist these children in achieving such goals.

OTHER STUDENTS

When a student is coping with a terminal illness, classmates are also affected. Many of the common grief reactions that are described in earlier chapters might arise for classmates of a child who is seriously or terminally ill. These include sadness, grief, anxiety, hopelessness, and confusion. Peers might also feel a sense of loss about no longer being able to count on the world being a safe, predictable place.

One of the best ways teachers can support students generally is by pursuing some of the anticipatory guidance activities that are described in this book. If students have already been learning about death and grief in the normal course of their schoolwork through lessons and teachable moments, they will be much better prepared to understand and cope with a classmate who is terminally ill. The school might identify a teacher known for being approachable on sensitive topics, such as death and grief, to be an ongoing resource for students dealing with this situation.

Teachers can also take specific steps when a student in their classroom is seriously ill. First, it is appropriate to check with the student's family to understand their wishes. Are they comfortable with the rest of the class knowing about their child's condition? How much may be disclosed? How much may be disclosed to students' families?

Ideally, families will agree that openness is the best policy, both for their child and for the other children in the school. Teachers may want to talk to families about the rationale for open communication on the subject. It creates a more natural and supportive setting for their child—one where classmates can comfortably offer support and their child can ask clearly for what he or she needs.

It is also important to check directly with the students who are seriously ill. How much information are they comfortable sharing at the classroom level? How would they like their classmates to learn of the situation? Do they want the teacher to make an announcement? Would they like to explain the situation themselves? Would they like one of their health care providers to come talk to the class? Would they be interested in a sort of question–answer session in which they can talk about their health condition and answer people's questions?

Some children who are terminally ill want a high level of involvement in telling their classmates. Some find it difficult because they are shy, do not feel well, or do not want to answer personal questions. The goal is to find an approach that works for each child and gives classmates sufficient background about the situation.

This raises the issue of what *is* sufficient information for the class. In general, students benefit by understanding something about the underlying condition, its treatment, and the side effects of treatment. A discussion of the possible side effects of treatment could include both observable effects, such as weight gain or fatigue, and those that are not so obvious, such as learning difficulties, confusion, irritability, pain that can lead the ill child to express frustration, and so forth. The complexity of this information should be adapted to match children's developmental level and understanding. Risk of transmission is also a concern for many students who may believe that cancer can be passed from person to person[6] or that HIV may be passed through usual classroom activities.[7] Teachers might also address the kind of support people with serious illness like to receive. Of course, the student who is ill can provide a helpful response to this question in particular.

The primary focus of these discussions should not be on death. It should be on the ways someone coping with a serious illness experiences his or her life. Nonetheless, children may at times ask directly or indirectly about the seriousness of the student's condition. The class can be told that the child's condition is serious, unlike many of the illnesses most children get that resolve quickly, with or without treatment. If it is consistent with the wishes of the student who is ill and his or her family, the class can be told that the medical team is doing everything possible to treat the condition but that generally, this condition is not curable. These conversations can obviously be very sensitive. Teachers should generally involve medical and/or mental health professionals in the classroom discussion.

It is also helpful to let the parents of other students know about these matters. Their children may have emotional responses to their classmate's illness, and they are likely to bring home questions and concerns. It would be helpful to provide parents basic facts about the affected student's condition, information about how the class learned about the situation, and guidance for talking with their children.

Parents should understand that this *is* a serious illness, different from most other illnesses that children experience. This can help them reassure their own children that they are not at significant risk for this or other serious illness. If treatment for the illness will have an effect on the child, it will be helpful for parents to understand what the side effects might be. It can also be helpful to give parents guidelines for talking about contagion so they can reassure their children that they will not catch this illness. Teachers may also want to refer parents to a reliable and informative web site or voluntary organization, such as the American Cancer Society, that provides additional background information.[8]

Some of these suggestions will be different for older students. Most high school students do not have a single class but instead, switch classes throughout the day. The school can work with the affected student and his or her family to find an approach that works. For example, a teen with a serious illness might ask that one or two classes deal with the matter more intensively. Or the teen might prefer to write a short announcement that is given by the teacher in each of his or her classes. Again, the goal is to explore different possibilities and find a solution that respects the student's wishes while providing appropriate support for all students.

Information for Parents of All Students

Information that may be helpful for parents of all students in the class includes

- The name of the illness or condition
- The fact that the illness is serious and different from most other illnesses children experience
- Ways to reassure children who may be anxious about contracting the condition themselves
- Treatment approaches and possible side effects
- Misconceptions their children may have (e.g., about contagion)
- A reliable resource for further information for parents (e.g., web site, voluntary organization)
- Reassurance of the commitment of the class and the school to continue to provide an excellent education for all of the students in the class

---

My Teacher Would Be Perfect at This!

Seven-year-old Miles had been experiencing some general weakness in his legs. His parents watched him struggle at times, and his teacher noticed this too. He could run, but not quite as quickly as the other students. He could play outdoor games and activities, but he became tired quickly. Sometimes his physical education class was difficult for him.

Miles's parents arranged a medical evaluation, and he was diagnosed with Duchenne muscular dystrophy (DMD). This is a progressive disorder that leads, over time, to severe muscular disability. Most children with DMD require a wheelchair by 12 years of age. Death often occurs in the teens or twenties. Miles's parents told the boy about his diagnosis so that he could understand more about his symptoms and the reason for all of the medical appointments and tests. They also spoke with his teacher about his condition and helped her plan appropriate classroom accommodations for their son.

Miles's classmates had also noticed his difficulties. They sometimes teased him for the slow pace of his running or for tiring out quickly. When he started a course of steroid treatments, he gained weight, and some children teased him about being fat. When teams were chosen for games, he was always one of the last chosen.

Miles talked to one of his doctors about these matters and decided that he would like his classmates to understand his condition. His mother had offered to come and talk to his class, but this idea embarrassed him. No one else's mother had come to the class to talk about her child. Miles didn't want his mother doing this.

The doctor suggested the boy could talk to the class himself. Miles didn't really feel that he knew enough about the condition because he was still learning about it. He was also quite shy, so standing up in front of the class sounded like a terrible idea to him.

The doctor then suggested that his mother give the background information to his teacher so that his teacher could talk to the class. Miles immediately brightened. "My teacher would be perfect at this!" he said enthusiastically. He turned to his mother in the middle of his clinic visit and said, "Can you call her right away?"

THE FAMILY OF A STUDENT WHO IS TERMINALLY ILL

As is true with families of grieving students, families of students who are terminally ill may turn to a trusted teacher for support and guidance. Teachers may want to initiate contact if they have not heard from a child's parents. As essential as it is for parents and teachers to talk, parents are often too overwhelmed at these times to initiate contact themselves. Teachers can offer suggestions that help a family cope with their feelings while providing the best possible support for their child. They can help parents identify resources for advice and support in the community or connect them with a mental health professional in the school who can provide specific recommendations.

About Siblings

The needs of siblings of a child who is seriously ill are often neglected. Parents, after all, have limited reserves of energy, time, and money. Their emotional resources are often stretched to the limit as their child's condition worsens. Teachers checking in with families can ask about siblings. Teachers who have the sibling of a child with a terminal illness in their class may find their involvement with the sibling to be critical to the child's academic success and emotional adjustment. The following are some suggestions of guidance to families:

- *A little attention can go a long way.* Many siblings understand the demands that parents are facing. Even a few moments of one-to-one attention can make a difference in the quality of their day. An occasional short walk together, a grocery store run, or an errand together can offer parents opportunities to stay connected to their other children.

- *Siblings should be informed about the ill child's health status and treatment plans.* Sometimes siblings are overlooked, especially when they are young. Parents may feel siblings would not understand what is happening or may simply feel they do not have the ability or time to explain it. This can leave siblings with the kind of anxiety that thrives around secrecy. What the child imagines might be happening is almost always worse than what is true.

  Siblings should understand that their brother or sister has a very serious illness. Once children who are terminally ill understand the seriousness of their condition, their siblings should be informed in an age-appropriate fashion as well. Siblings should also be given an opportunity to participate in the care of the ill child. Young children may be given simple tasks, such as bringing in cards from the mail and opening them, watering plants in the room, or bringing toys to a child in bed.

  It is important not to overload siblings with unreasonable chores or responsibilities, especially older children and adolescents. Continued involvement in activities outside the family—peer groups, sports teams, after-school activities—is a valuable source of support for siblings, especially because support at home may be limited.

- *Siblings respond to these situations with the same range of emotions that adults do.* Siblings may be angry at the ill child for receiving all of the attention or for abandoning them. They may feel guilty about being healthy and surviving, or they may believe that they are responsible for the illness in some way. They may feel hopeless, sad, or confused about what to do to support their sibling.

- *School support is important.* Siblings' teachers should be informed of the family situation. School staff can make an extra effort to reach out to siblings of children who are terminally or seriously ill. Teachers of siblings can also play a critical role in giving them support at a time when their families may have limited resources, time, and energy. Teachers can watch for any signs of troubled behavior, and if a sibling has significant changes in academic or social behavior, a referral to counseling would be appropriate. Families may feel more reassured if they know that school staff are expressing special interest in the siblings.

  Some hospitals, clinics, hospice programs, disease-specific support groups or organizations, and schools provide programs or family support groups that are open to siblings of children with chronic or serious medical problems. School mental health or medical staff such as the school nurse, family pediatrician, or other health care provider may know of these resources.

Working with a student who is terminally ill is one of the most stressful personal and professional experiences a teacher can face. It is important for teachers to seek out resources for support. Strategies that teachers can use for their own support are described in Chapter 12.

ENDNOTES

1. Schonfeld and Lewis (2005).
2. Glazer and Schonfeld (2007).
3. Greenham and Lohmann (1982).
4. Spinetta (1974).
5. Clunies-Ross and Lansdown (1988).
6. Chin, Schonfeld, O'Hare, Mayne, Salovey, et al.(1998).
7. Schonfeld, Johnson, Perrin, O'Hare, and Cicchetti (1993).
8. A web site prepared by elementary school children to educate children about cancer can be found at http://info.med.yale.edu/ycc/kidsinfo/

11
Memorialization
and Commemoration

It is natural for people to want to remember, honor, and reflect on those who have died. We do these things through funerals, events that commemorate the deceased, the placements of memorial markers, and similar activities.

When a member of the school community dies, there is also a need to acknowledge the death. However, considerations in school settings are somewhat different from those in private ones. The choices schools make will have an impact on a large number of students and staff in the present *and* in the future. They also have an impact on the family of the person who died.

Careful thought and planning about appropriate general policies before a death occurs allows schools to make the best possible decisions for their settings and communities. A number of guidelines will help these activities provide meaningful and positive support for students, staff, and families.

GOALS OF
MEMORIALIZATION AND COMMEMORATION

Death can be confusing to survivors. Why did it happen? Why is it so painful? What is the purpose of life if this is all it comes to? One of the reasons we have memorializations and commemorations is to provide a context in which survivors can begin to find answers to these questions. Typically, survivors find some meaning and purpose in the life of those who died. We remember something special they did, a contribution they made, or a way our life was changed because we knew them. We are reminded by their death that life is precious—a gift to be appreciated every day. We make our own commitments to do more to help others, be true to ourselves, reach our goals, or appreciate our lives.

Children can find helpful support through commemorative activities.[1] These activities or events help them express and cope with difficult feelings that might otherwise seem overwhelming to them. They can draw on the support of a caring community—their peers, teachers, and school- or community-based counseling staff. They can learn from others who are also facing these challenging feelings, and everyone can share techniques for coping. A commemorative activity can give children a framework for further discussion with their parents or other family members.

Commemorations in school settings do not need to be elaborate. Often a brief and simple activity is all that is needed. This might be a short class discussion about the ways that students want to remember the person who died. When schools do plan a more structured memorial, the process will be most helpful if the following guidelines are kept in mind.

GIVING STUDENTS A VOICE

It is vital that students have a role in planning how to commemorate a classmate, teacher, or other member of the school community who has died. The event that is actually planned is far less important than *how* it is planned. When children take the lead, they can suggest activities that are relevant to their circumstances and developmental needs. They will think of activities that have meaning to them—and these sometimes are not the same things that have meaning to adults. Children have many creative and unique ideas, and they often think of things adults do not.

It is more productive for children to remember someone in a way that they have chosen and that has meaning for them than it is to walk mechanically through a ritual someone else has selected. By choosing an activity or a ceremony that speaks to them, children are putting effective ways to cope with their grief directly into practice. They and their classmates are modeling coping together. They are learning about positive ways to deal with grief that will serve them in their future lives.

Children are also taking some measure of control in a situation that might otherwise leave them feeling quite powerless. They may not have been able to prevent the death. They may not be able to stop their own feelings of sadness. However, choosing what they want most to remember and how they want to express that remembrance is an important way for them to experience greater self-determination. Going through this process can help them master some of the difficult feelings that accompany grief.

Another important reason for involving children in planning a commemorative activity is that when this is not done, students often come up with their own means of memorialization. Under some circumstances, these informal memorials can pose problems (see Spontaneous Memorials later in this chapter).

Planting Flowers

When a fourth-grade student died, the school organized a memorial assembly for her classmates and others who had known her. The principal and several teachers spoke to the group about their classmate. The adults remembered what a kind child she had been and how much she had enjoyed helping others. They reminded the students of how much she had enjoyed nature and gardens.

At the end of the assembly, the principal told the students that they were all going to go outside and plant flowers in the garden as a special way to remember their classmate. The children formed a line and each was given a small flower to plant. They went outside and found the flower bed prepared and ready. The teachers helped them put the flowers into the soil. The students stood back and watched as one of the gardeners carefully watered the newly planted flowers. Then they returned to their class.

The principal and teachers found the planting of the flowers quite emotional. The students, however, were not as moved by the activity. This wasn't the thing that they remembered most about their classmate. They weren't entirely sure what the flowers had to do with their friend's death. During the assembly, they hadn't been able to express their feelings or hear from one another about how they were coping with the loss. Although they politely went through the motions of planting their flowers, the activity did not give them a greater sense of control in the situation or a deeper understanding of their own feelings.

Although the flower planting was clearly a useful symbol for the adults involved in this memorial, it was of little help for the students themselves. They would have been better served by an activity they had chosen that allowed them to acknowledge and express their own feelings.

HELPING STUDENTS PLAN A POSITIVE ACTIVITY

Teachers, school counselors, or other school staff can help children plan an activity that makes sense for students. A good start is engaging them in a discussion that explores their feelings and gives direction to their plans. Teachers and school administrators often worry that such discussions, or the commemorative activities themselves, will upset students. Of course, it is the death of someone they know and care about that is the true source of distress, not these conversations about it. Having the conversation also allows teachers to observe what students are feeling and thinking. It is better for these things to be out in the open, where children can receive support, than for children to feel they need to keep their feelings hidden.

These conversations work best when staff facilitate open-ended discussions with students. Asking questions and listening to answers provides much useful information. It is important to avoid the temptation to tell students how they should be feeling about the death. Although adults can offer suggestions, especially to initiate the conversation for younger children, the children themselves should suggest their own ideas and choose the approach they believe will best express their feelings and facilitate remembrance.

Some questions that teachers and staff can ask to start the conversation may include the following:

- *What do you remember about the person who died?* This question provides a wide-open palette for children to remember and remind each other of the things that were important to them. In a fully open discussion, students might include both positive and negative qualities about the person, or some unpleasant memories about the person's illness or the way that he or she died.

- *What do you want to remember about the person?* This allows children to filter through their memories and focus on those that are positive.

- *What are some ways we could take time to observe or mark these remembrances?* Let students suggest a range of ideas. Some may be completely impractical, whereas others may be movingly poignant. Often, students come up with ideas that are both pragmatic and simple—a 10-minute remembrance in which students can say a few words if they wish or a picture that the group makes for the family of the person who died.

Once several ideas are on the table, students can work with their teacher or other staff to select those that seem best in their situation. This gives students the opportunity to share their ideas and feelings in the group, to come to a shared understanding about the commemorative activity, and to collectively identify a meaningful and helpful way to commemorate the person who died. When students can participate in planning and carrying out their own ideas, the results are likely to have greater relevance for them. The following story is a good example.

What Shall We Do with His Desk?

Two schools experienced similar tragedies. In each case, a child found a gun, played with it, and accidentally discharged it. In both instances, a second-grade student was killed. In each classroom, the surviving students were confused and troubled about what to do with the desk of the student who died.

No one wanted to sit at it. No one wanted it removed because that would feel like they were ignoring their classmate. No one wanted it sitting there empty because every time they came into their classroom they all looked right at the empty desk and remembered the tragic circumstances of their classmate's death.

Clearly, something needed to be done to symbolize each class's grief, sense of remembrance, and commitment to move forward. But what would it be?

In each case, the students themselves came up with a solution, but each class came up with a different idea. Both of these ideas worked well for their particular class.

In the first class, the students all talked about what they wanted to remember about the student who had died. They decided they wanted to honor his strengths. He had been a good reader who loved books and encouraged other students to read. They chose to move his desk to a corner in the back of the classroom and place a selection of books on the desk. Students with free time could sit at the desk. They could read a book of their own or choose one from those placed on the desk. They could remember their classmate while they improved their skills at reading—something they all knew he would appreciate.

In the second class, the students decided to clear all of the desks in the room of personal possessions. They stacked all of their books, papers, and pencils on their chairs. The janitors came into the class that night and scrubbed all of the desks clean. Then they rearranged them so no desk was in the same place it had originally been.

The next day, students went back to their chairs and saw before them a freshly scrubbed, thoroughly cleaned desk. The desk of the student who had died was among them, but no one knew exactly where. They liked knowing his desk was still part of the classroom. As they filled their "new" desks with their possessions, all of the students had a sense that they were making a fresh start.

When choosing how to commemorate a student who died, students and teachers can consider some of the hallmarks of a positive commemorative activity. These may include some of the following:

- *The activity makes sense to students.* The commemorative activities speak to their interests, needs, and memories of the deceased. Participants have an opportunity to feel their grief, try to make sense of what has happened, and feel hopeful about the future.

- *An opportunity is provided for students to share coping techniques with their peers.* Some part of the planning, the commemoration, or the discussion afterward includes students sharing feelings that they have had in response to the death and how they are coping with these feelings.

- *Students' emotional lives are respected.* A wide range of emotions is a normal part of grief. Students should understand that it is okay to have strong feelings —or to not have them. Students can be encouraged to talk about the things they are thinking and feeling before, during, or after the commemoration. Support should be available to students who wish to talk with a counselor about their responses, either in the period immediately after the death or many months into the future.

- *There is a focus on helping students learn to manage and cope with their feelings about this and other losses.* From these experiences, students understand that when people have strong feelings related to grief or other issues, they can take steps to receive support.

- *The function and purpose of the school is kept uppermost—learning, education, and promoting well-being and health.* Informed schools understand that the death of a student or staff member will have a profound effect on some members of the school community. Such schools provide support for the school as a whole as well as individual students and staff. They understand that grief can be distracting and challenging. They respect the grief process and the needs of the school community. They also keep focused on their primary functions. They return to usual routines and a focus on learning as soon as they reasonably and sensitively can.

CHALLENGES FOR SCHOOLS

Schools face a number of challenges in planning and managing commemorative activities and formal memorializations. These are the sorts of issues that are best dealt with proactively, before a death occurs. For example,

- *Some events might glamorize risky or self-destructive behaviors.* If a student has died by suicide, other vulnerable students may find the attention of memorialization appealing. A student who feels isolated or depressed might think, "I'd like to be remembered this way," or "I wonder if the people who have ignored me would feel as sad if I died." Students may have similar thoughts about a fellow student who was a victim of a gang-related killing. Attention given to the death might inadvertently glamorize gang violence or play a role in provoking retaliation.

Memorials for a student who died while engaging in other risky behaviors might also make these activities more tempting. This could include such things as a drug overdose, drag racing, a game of chicken, or climbing to the top of a local landmark.

- *Students may be confused about what is expected.* If students did not know the deceased well, they may be uncertain about how much to say, what they are supposed to feel, and whether they are obligated to participate in a ceremony. If they *did* know the person who died well, they may feel that some aspects of a broadly drawn memorial trivialize the death, and that people who did not care much for the person in life seem to be using the death as a way to draw attention to themselves. Students who did not get along with the deceased may feel it is inauthentic to participate in a remembrance but feel pressured to do so.

- *Precedents are set.* When a student is remembered in an official school capacity, a precedent is set. If a school goes all out to memorialize a popular student who dies tragically in a car crash, what steps will it take a year later when a lesser known student dies? If something less is done, what message is given to that student's family and friends or to other quiet, less well-known students in the school?

  Furthermore, what is done about students who die while engaging in risky or illegal activities? What about a student who dies of suicide? Situations quickly become complicated if all memorializations are not similar in scope.

- *Markers, plaques, or other memorials often send mixed messages.* Markers to memorialize students who have died can also lead to challenges. If a marker is placed for one student who dies, a precedent is set. If another student subsequently dies of suicide, a marker might glamorize that death and would not be appropriate.

  Some memorialization approaches are more likely to disturb students than console them. For example, if many students in a community have died by violence, and a school memorializes them by planting a tree in a special "peace grove" each time a student dies, what do students see in these trees? Are they constantly reminded that they live in a neighborhood of extreme violence, and that many of their classmates are not living to adulthood? Instead of helping them cope with their grief and move forward in their lives, the trees may feel more like a body count. Students might wonder when their own trees will be planted.

  Markers might also be vandalized, damaged accidently, or fall into disrepair. This can be painful to the family of the deceased, and it can also communicate a sense of disrespect for the deceased.

GUIDELINES FOR RECOGNIZING AND REMEMBERING

Some schools have established policies for recognizing and remembering students or staff who have died. Policies can help schools encourage planning appropriate commemorative activities—those that benefit students and staff and help them cope with their grief. When policies or guidelines are in place, they can also help schools avoid some of the common difficulties with memorialization that were just described.

Memorial and Funeral Services

Chapter 3 discusses some of the reasons it is helpful for children to attend the funerals of friends and family members. When a death touches an entire school, however, the question of how to plan for student and staff attendance becomes larger.

Schools should check with the family of the deceased to see if they have any wishes about students or staff attending the service. If many people in the school knew the deceased, students and staff may be able to participate in visitation outside of school hours. Ideally, the service itself would also be scheduled for a time when school is not in session. This helps minimize disruption of the school's schedule. It also makes it easier for students to attend with their families, which is generally the best choice for children and teens attending funerals or memorial services.

If the service is during school hours, schools may want to set a policy about student absences. For example, students who had a close relationship to the deceased and have permission from their parents may be excused to attend. Substitute teachers can be arranged for teachers and other school staff who wish to attend. It might also be helpful to have counseling staff present at a memorial or funeral service that is likely to be attended by many students. Counseling staff will also be helpful at the school after the service.

Attendance at services should be completely voluntary. Sometimes students feel pressured to attend services even if it is not what they want to do. If regular classes can go forward as scheduled, they should. Students who have missed class activities to attend a funeral may need some extra help catching up on assignments or going over the content of missed classwork.

Spontaneous Memorials

Informal memorials often "spring up" after the death of a student or teacher. People might place flowers, notes, photos, books, stuffed animals, and other sentimental items somewhere on the school grounds. The memorials might also involve graffiti on walls, walkways, or lockers.

There is not necessarily anything wrong with informal memorials, and students and staff may find them helpful. However, it is important for schools to place limits as appropriate and quickly determine how long such a memorial is left in place. Usually a few days to a week is appropriate.

The school should communicate the plan to students (e.g., "The memorial will be removed on Friday afternoon."). Let students know what will be done with nonperishable items (e.g., stuffed animals might be donated to the thrift shop of a local charity). They may also communicate what contributions are acceptable, such as letters, notes, and photos, but clarify that graffiti on school property is not allowed. Students should be invited to check with administrators or school counselors if they have any questions or concerns about the memorial.

Sometimes the management of informal memorials can be a problem. They should be monitored regularly in case something inappropriate is placed at the site (e.g., a bottle of beer, a suggestive photograph). They should also be checked to ensure that students do not post harmful messages. For example, after a student has died by suicide, someone might write a message that says, "You made the right decision." If someone died in a gang-related incident, a message might say, "I'll find the person who did this and make sure he joins you." In other cases, students may contribute messages that are negative or critical about the person who died. They might say, "You were a jerk," or "This couldn't have happened to a better person. I'm glad you're gone." These are obviously hurtful and inappropriate and need to be removed.

Providing alternative commemorative opportunities for students and engaging them early on in planning the response efforts may help minimize interest in informal memorials. Students may benefit from creative writing projects addressing their feelings about such things as the person who died, losses they have experienced, or how to remember people we care for who have died. Art projects or other creative endeavors may also help student express their thoughts and feelings.

Guidelines for Spontaneous Memorials

Some guidelines that schools have found helpful include

- Set a reasonable length for the memorials to be in place, usually a few days to a week. Communicate the plan to students.

- Ensure that objects placed at the memorial do not interfere with access to lockers, classrooms, stairs, walkways, or emergency exits. Work with students to identify an alternate site if necessary. Usual safety standards should be maintained.

- Let students know that content will be monitored and inappropriate objects or messages will be removed.

- Invite students to check with administrators or school counselors if they have any questions about or responses to the memorial.

- Monitor the memorial regularly throughout the day. Remove inappropriate material.

TIMING OF COMMEMORATIVE ACTIVITIES AT SCHOOL

In the immediate aftermath of a death, the focus should be on notifying students and staff and providing them with opportunities to receive emotional support. It is important to give the school community a certain amount of time and space in which to notice and understand their emotions and thoughts about the death. Deaths of members of the school community are major events. Their impact takes time to emerge.

Activities to memorialize someone who has died can begin too quickly. Steps such as raising money for a scholarship fund to honor a teacher who died are sometimes begun within hours, or even minutes, of the death being announced. When this happens, energy is diverted from the immediate emotional experiences that students and staff are having. People often get the sense that emotional closure is expected rapidly. This discourages children and adults from experiencing their emotions fully. Students, staff, parents, or the community in general may feel the school is rushing to "close the chapter" on grieving.

Commemorative activities or reminders that go on too long, however, can also be a problem for students and staff. Feelings of sadness or confusion may be prolonged instead of being allowed to gradually decrease in intensity. Students or staff may get the impression that they are expected to continue to express the loss in an immediate and powerful way, even if this is not authentically what they are feeling.

Although there is no "right" framework of time for personal bereavement, the overall goal for the school is to recognize the death, remember the deceased, respect the feelings of the school community, *and* move forward in a sensitive way with their main function—the education of children.

Sometimes conflicts arise about the type or length of a memorial effort. The family of a student who died, or the student's closest friends, will feel the loss more deeply. They might wish for a more constant reminder, such as a marker, photos, or a semipermanent installation of flowers or candles. Other students or staff might feel distracted by persistent reminders of an event that did not affect them as deeply. Even students who were close to the deceased may be confused by a protracted memorial process. When these efforts are sustained for a long time, they may give children the impression that they must continue to hold on to their grief as a way to maintain their memory of the person who died.

This is not the message that should be given to children or the model that should be provided. This is why, in school settings, it is important to establish mechanisms by which different members of the school community can express their needs and views on how to best meet these needs and, as a community, reach a respectful compromise. This might include students and their families, administrators, teachers, school mental health staff, and other school staff. Staff can also determine the wishes of the family of the deceased and communicate these to the school community. This will usually lead to a more effective process than having a single administrator make all the necessary decisions.

Our Boy's Favorite Toy

Gilbert, a student in the kindergarten class, died suddenly, shortly before the winter holidays. He was an only child, and his parents, who had filled their lives with his interests and activities, were devastated by his death.

The children in his class were told of the death, as were other students in the school. The kindergarten teacher and one of the school counselors worked closely with the children and their families during this time to make sure the students understood what had happened and felt comfortable expressing their feelings about it. They all seemed to be managing well.

When the school presented its annual holiday concert, the kindergarten class sang a beautiful winter song. Gilbert's parents came to see the concert and brought along their son's favorite toy—a small plush bunny with floppy ears. They chose their seats in the auditorium and sat the bunny on the seat between them.

All of the families around them noticed, and some were moved to tears. A few spoke to the parents after the event and said how glad they were to see them there. Many of the children in Gilbert's class were saddened when they saw the boy's parents and his favorite toy. A few cried. A couple of the children said they felt bad having the concert because now they were remembering their classmate. Their teacher reassured them that the concert was a good thing to do and did not in any way take away from their feelings about their classmate.

In February, the kindergarten class had a special event for President's Day. Students told stories about Abraham Lincoln and George Washington and sang patriotic songs. Then they had apples and punch. Some of the parents attended. Gilbert's parents appeared, once more bringing their son's bunny and giving it a seat. Again, some of the children were upset. Should they be celebrating President's Day? Was it right to have a party? The teacher overheard two of the students talking about the toys their parents would bring if *they* died.

At the end of the year, the class was planning its graduation. By this time, the teacher was uncomfortable with what she called "the bunny situation." She saw that it was distressing the children and thought this ongoing reminder of Gilbert's death was not helpful. A few of her students' parents had also raised the issue. She asked the principal to speak with Gilbert's parents.

The principal did not agree. "These parents have lost their child. These simple events obviously offer them some degree of comfort. Can't we just give this to them? They have lost so much."

The parents came to kindergarten graduation, and the bunny came along.

This pattern continued as the children grew older. The bunny came to winter and spring concerts, school fairs, and other special events. As the years went by, Gilbert's former classmates were reminded of him each time they achieved something themselves. New students came into the school who had not known Gilbert. "What's with the bunny?" they would ask. "Oh, you'll get used to him," other students would answer.

In a sense, however, the students did not really "get used to" the bunny. It continued to be a reminder to them that they had moved forward while the boy the bunny represented stayed frozen in time. The parents showed them an immobile state of grief—unable to make true meaning in their lives without their son's presence. These children were burdened unfairly, compelled to continue carrying grief for this child they had known only briefly and long ago. It was not a healthy way to model and practice bereavement.

The bunny situation ended after sixth-grade graduation. At that point, the children moved on to a larger school. The principal had never quite been able to tell the parents that the bunny had become a disturbing reminder, not an honorable remembrance, of their son. If the school had established a different process for making decisions, this situation could have been resolved early on before it became a problem for the students. For example, the school crisis team, which usually includes mental health staff, teachers, and administrators, could have worked through the situation with the principal. Together, they would most likely have found a better solution to this difficult and delicate situation.

MONITORING EXPRESSIONS OF GRIEF

Sometimes students wish to write letters or draw pictures to send to the family of the deceased. It is important that these are reviewed before they are sent out to make sure they are appropriate and will not be disturbing to the family. It is also possible that some students will express troublesome thoughts, such as feelings of despair and hopelessness or thoughts of suicide.

It is not usually helpful for teachers or school administrators to interpret students' drawings or writing—these assessments take specialized experience and training. However, if they observe content that raises concerns, it would be prudent and wise to ask a mental health professional in the school to review the materials and, if indicated, speak with the student who produced them. It is not unusual for a death to bring up painful memories or thoughts, and written or drawn expressions of grief can be the outlet that brings these forward.

We recommend against activities that solicit anonymous statements, such as posting large pieces of paper where students can write out their thoughts and comments about the deceased. Some students have written disturbing comments in such activities—threatening suicide or harm to others, for example—and school staff cannot identify these students to intervene. In some instances, especially after posts have been up for a few days, critical or negative comments about the deceased have appeared. This is damaging for everyone in the school. Such posts should be removed immediately if they do appear.

AFFIRMING A RANGE OF RESPONSES

When someone in the school community dies, students and staff will have a range of responses. Some individuals will be closer to the person who died than others. Some will have a stronger identification with the person. Some will have other problems in their lives that have been creating a burden and may be especially vulnerable to powerful feelings of anxiety or sadness when they learn of the death.

Some may have little emotional response at all, perhaps only a cordial concern for the surviving family members or a passing sadness that someone has died.

It is important to affirm this full range of expressions when talking to students about their feelings. Just as we cannot predict with certainty who, in a group of students, may be deeply affected by a death, we cannot know the students for whom the death will have little impact.

Children should not feel pressured or coerced into showing their grief. The goal, after all, is to support them in having authentic feelings and thoughts and to give them guidance to move along in the process at a pace that is appropriate for them. If children feel as if there is a particular way they are supposed to act or something they are supposed to do, they will not be learning anything useful about grief, loss, or managing their own emotions.

Am I Supposed to Go to the Funeral?

Cheyenne, a middle school student, was saddened to learn one Monday morning that the mother of one of her classmates had died over the weekend. She didn't know the girl well, but she had no trouble imagining that this was an extremely painful experience.

The girl's friends wanted to find ways to support her. "The funeral is tomorrow," they told Cheyenne. "We're all wearing purple that day as a sign of our support. And we need to get permission from our parents to leave school early to go to the funeral. Don't forget!"

Cheyenne was confused. She had great sympathy for the girl, but she wasn't a close friend. She had never met the mother. She didn't know the family.

She also didn't have anything purple to wear—she never liked the color. Was she supposed to go buy something to wear the next day? Was she supposed to get permission from her parents to go to the funeral of someone she didn't know? She hadn't been to a funeral before, and it seemed odd and sort of dishonest to her to contemplate going to this one.

Many of Cheyenne's friends were planning to attend the funeral. What would they think of her, she wondered, if she showed up in another color? What if she skipped the funeral? Would they think she was stuck up? Would she be left out of social events in the future if she didn't participate?

Cheyenne liked her English teacher a lot. After class, Cheyenne asked her what she thought she should do. Her teacher assured her that she did not need to attend the funeral, and that she should only take steps that felt honest and authentic to her. She encouraged Cheyenne to talk to her parents about her concerns.

Cheyenne did talk to her parents, and, with their help, they came up with a solution. First, she let her friends know that she wasn't going to attend the funeral, and she explained why. They were disappointed, but accepted her explanation. Then she asked her mother to help her choose an outfit for school. They found one that felt both comfortable and true for Cheyenne—a simple black t-shirt and black slacks. She attended classes as usual and wished her friends well as they departed for the funeral service.

When the girl whose mother died returned to school a week later, Cheyenne approached her and said, "I was sorry to hear about your mother's death." The girl smiled and thanked her.

HANDLING TRAUMATIC REMINDERS

Sometimes, planned memorial events heighten traumatic reminders of the person who died or the event that led to the death. The goal of memorialization is for students to remember what was lost and what they wish to preserve about their relationship with the deceased. This is not the same as remembering the details of the death itself.

When possible, it is best to minimize traumatic reminders of the actual event. For example, a moment of silence during morning announcements to remember a classmate who died on the playground may be helpful. However, scheduling that moment of silence to occur during a special gathering on the playground near the site of the death and at the same time of day the incident occurred has a greater risk of retraumatizing students.

School desks and lockers may also serve as unwelcome and painful reminders of the deceased student. Schools should solicit input from students and staff about how to handle these matters. Some examples were discussed earlier in the chapter.

SUPPORT FOR THE FAMILY

In addition to commemoration or memorialization, it is also helpful for schools to think through the types of contacts they will have with the family of a student or staff member who has died. For example, schools will want to arrange the return of the deceased's personal effects to parents or family members. Students can be told that their classmate's belongings are going to be returned to the family. The materials can be gathered together, typically outside of regular school hours, and made available at the office so that the parents do not have to go through the emotional challenge of cleaning out their child's desk or locker. This exchange may take place after school hours to protect both the family and the students. We recommend that a member of the school crisis response team or counseling staff be available as well to provide support to the family.

The family should also be removed from the school mailing list as appropriate (i.e., if no siblings are in the school), so that the family does not inadvertently receive routine mailings.

MOVING FORWARD AS A COMMUNITY

One of the overarching goals of all of these commemorative efforts is to keep the school on track doing what schools do—caring for children's well-being and providing their education. Each situation is different, and the goal is not to establish hard-and-fast rules that are rigidly applied, but to come up with a process that involves the input of interested parties with appropriate expertise—administrators, school mental health staff, students, and teachers. A policy can be established that supports the process.

Ultimately, the way each person is remembered by friends, teachers, peers, or colleagues depends on the particular situation. This includes who the person was, what caused the death, and what people feel they want to do in response. It is important that memorialization in different situations is equitable and fair. This does not mean they must always be the same.

It is also helpful to remember that school communities that come together to support each other and commemorate one of their members who has died are often brought closer together by the experience. The death of a student or staff member can be transformative for students, their families, staff, and the school community as a whole. Teachers who understand the importance of giving children appropriate guidance and assistance at such times are in an ideal position to support such possibilities. The best outcome of the transformation is a return to a sense of normalcy, however. Studies move forward, information is learned, and students and staff alike know themselves a little more deeply than they did before.

ENDNOTES

1. See Schonfeld (2002).

12
Taking Care of Yourself

When teachers and schools take the steps outlined in this book, they help bereaved students in some of the most important ways possible. They can offer families advice and support that help them cope with their own grief while supporting their children. Through anticipatory guidance and teaching, they can also help all students develop a deeper understanding about death, loss, compassion, and how to be supportive of a grieving friend. They can model for students the ways people can reach out to others in time of need. They can help establish a sense of community in their own class, one where class members care about one another and express this in words and actions.

Teachers can reap the benefits, as well. Most teachers go into teaching because they want to help children learn and grow. There are few better ways to do this than to help students cope with one of the most difficult challenges of their lives. It is gratifying to reach students by understanding their needs and helping them better understand themselves.

Teachers who make these efforts often find they can connect with their students in a qualitatively different manner. They touch students' lives in powerful and meaningful ways, helping them realize that adults around them can and do care. Quite often, just a small amount of effort, which may be associated with a bit of initial discomfort on the teacher's part, can have a significant impact on students. Ultimately, this can be very uplifting for teachers. It is quite gratifying to realize that a small amount of work can play a role in helping children manage these difficult situations and minimize the time in which they feel isolated, confused, and distressed.

Clearly, many teachers feel somewhat unprepared or apprehensive about addressing topics such as death, however. Some are afraid that if they reach out to a grieving student, they will do the wrong thing or start something they will not know how to complete. Sometimes, teachers may be so moved by a particular student or family's situation that they find they want to extend themselves a bit further. This can be difficult to manage, given teachers' already busy days.

Another possible difficulty, which was mentioned previously, is that once students know they can approach a teacher on difficult matters, they may want to talk about other challenges in their lives. Such teachers may receive more requests from both students and colleagues to respond to children's needs about bereavement, difficult family situations, conflicts with friends, or a wide range of other matters. When too many of these requests are focused on one teacher, he or she is likely to feel overburdened by the demands.

One of the best solutions to all of these issues is to train teachers broadly in this area. Talking with children about grief should not be the special province of one or two teachers, but something that many teachers feel prepared to do. Training helps teachers build skills, ensures that schools have many staff prepared to help grieving students, and strengthens the emotional support that allows teachers to do this work well. Teachers can also think carefully about how confident they feel doing this work, as well as how much they are able to offer in terms of practical matters such as time and emotional energy (see Preparation: Ready to Help Students later in this chapter).

I Care and Want to Help

Paul, a 7-year-old student, was participating in a study about ways children understand death and experience loss. He had given a response to an interviewer named Laura that raised concerns. She spoke with the head of the study, who worked at the school as a consultant. This individual followed up by requesting a private meeting with Paul. The teacher released the student from class so that he could attend the meeting. Paul came in and said hello. He recognized the man because he had talked to Paul's class earlier about death and grief.

The consultant said, "I was concerned about something you said when you spoke to Laura last week. It made us wonder if something was bothering you, and if there was anything we could do to help."

Paul looked surprised, and then he started to cry. Yes, he was troubled. His father was abusing cocaine. It was getting worse every day. He wanted someone to make sure his father would be okay and that he would not die. He worried about this all of the time.

As the consultant continued talking with Paul, it became clear that this *wasn't* the same Paul who had given the troubling response to Laura. A substitute teacher who didn't know the students' last names had sent the wrong boy. Yet, this student, essentially chosen at random, was simply told someone cared and wanted to help. He revealed some deeply troubling events in his life.

Children carry to school feelings related to big problems every day. They deal with homelessness, parental substance abuse, community violence, bullying in school, and a host of other concerns. Teachers identified as trustworthy resources for support may discover many challenging things about their students.

Teachers do not need to solve all of these problems; however, having resources on hand that can lend support is helpful. If children do not receive support for their concerns, it will be difficult for them to concentrate on their work and make true progress at school.

COMMON REACTIONS FOR TEACHERS

Teachers come up with a number of personal themes when the NCSCB trains teachers and works with those who are dealing with bereaved students. The following section outlines some of the most common issues, as well as suggestions about how to respond.

Triggers for Personal Grief

Few teachers have not been touched in some way by grief and loss. Most have experienced the death of a friend or family member. Any time people are exposed to others' grief, it can act as a trigger for their own past experiences. This is one reason people cry at movies or manage to "keep it together" at a funeral until they see someone else crying. It is not surprising that talking with a student about the death of someone he or she loved could trigger a teacher's grief.

These triggers can be even more powerful if the death affecting a student is in some way similar to an important loss the teacher has also experienced. Teachers who lost a parent while young may feel a student's loss of a parent quite deeply. Someone whose father died of cancer may feel more deeply affected by a student whose father died the same way.

Having to explain death to children requires that teachers put into words things any of us may find hard to acknowledge—their family member or friend or classmate is dead and will never be back. Once someone we love dies, we will never see that person again. It is quite likely that we will miss the person for the rest of our lives. This reminds teachers of people they have lost and the reality that they, too, will continue to miss those people.

The following are suggestions for handling grief triggers:

- Recognize that grief triggers are common reactions and a typical feature of the lifelong process of grief.

- Keep personal grief reactions separate from students' experiences. A student's reactions will be unique. Even if a teacher has similar experiences, he or she cannot know what the student is going through. Keep asking questions and listening.

- Monitor personal reactions. If the grief of a student is particularly difficult, teachers should seek support from others. They should talk about their feelings with someone they trust.

- Consider delegating some of the work of supporting a student to a colleague who is not as personally affected. This support can be repaid in the same, or different, way at another time.

Concern About the Support Grieving Students Receive from Their Families

We probably all have a picture in our mind of the "perfect" supportive setting for children and families to cope with grief. However, what teachers see in reality is often less than perfect. Some families do not have the simple resources that many of us take for granted—caring friends, extended family, the ability to read a book on grieving. We might come up with a dozen good suggestions for receiving support, none of which are practical for a particular family at that point in time. At these incredibly stressful moments, good parents may not be at their best. Parents who are already challenged by mental illness, substance abuse, health issues, or other matters may be even less able to support their children.

Furthermore, in grief, people may say impulsive or careless things. They may not identify or understand their children's needs well. They may be overwhelmed with their own grief or sadness and be unable to attend to their children fully.

One of the most common—and reasonable—reactions teachers have is concern about the type of support students can receive from their families. The following are some suggestions for these situations:

- Recognize that witnessing grief in families can be stressful.

- Find others with whom to share feelings and responses.

- Recognize the limits of a teacher's role. Most teachers must already do this when they become aware of some of the challenges facing their students. Grief may demand even greater than usual skill in this.

- Seek additional support if necessary. This might include identifying referrals for students and their families (see Chapters 6 and 7), talking with a colleague, or receiving consultation personally (see the Receiving and Giving Support section later in this chapter).

Discomfort

Many aspects of supporting grieving children can be challenging. Some teachers are uncomfortable talking or thinking about death. Some are frustrated that they cannot do more for their students. Some feel anxious for their students. Some feel angry about the events that led to a student's suffering—perhaps a sense of unfairness about the death or the inability of a student's family to provide appropriate support.

Witnessing the grief of a child or adolescent can be difficult. Adults sense a particular vulnerability in children and want to protect them from harsh and painful experiences. Symbolically, children often represent innocence, and many adults are touched by children's ability to be positive and hopeful in a difficult world. Watching a child struggle to cope with the death of a parent or other family member or friend—and lose that innocence about a benevolent world—can be particularly heart wrenching.

These feelings can be quite strong at times, and they are not comfortable. The following are two suggestions for handling this discomfort:

- Recognize that witnessing children's grief can be uncomfortable. This is a common reaction.

- Seek support from others. Teachers should talk about their feelings with some-one they trust.

Resentment

Many demands are placed on teachers. They often feel that they are being asked to do too many things for students without adequate support or compensation. There are few other professions that ask for as much with so little recognition. If this is the baseline for a teacher, and then he or she is asked to do even more for bereaved students, feelings of resentment might understandably emerge. Resentment is most likely to occur when teachers feel they are expected to do something they have not been prepared for, are not supported in, or do not have the time to do. They may feel that they are just being given more work to be done, more time to spend, more skills to learn—and that the work is emotionally challenging in the bargain.

The following are some suggestions for handling resentment:

- Proactively support trainings for staff on helping children cope with grief. When more staff know these skills, the burden can be shared and resentments are less likely to arise.
- Be conscious of personal feelings and reactions. If resentment comes up, recognize that it is a common and understandable response.
- If possible, set aside the feelings of resentment while interacting with students.
- If the feelings persist and the teacher is unable to set aside feelings of resentment in a way that allows for offering genuine support to a student, it is necessary to identify another staff member who can be a support to the student.
- Seek support from others. Teachers should talk about their feelings with some-one they trust. They can also consider talking with a consultant.

Guilt

Guilt is another uncomfortable but understandable reaction that teachers sometimes have. They might feel guilty because they are resentful about the extra work and effort it takes to support grieving students (e.g., "How can I feel resentful when my student is suffering so much more than I am?"). They might feel guilty because they do not feel that they are spending enough time with a bereaved student. They might feel guilty because a bereaved student is coping with a level of suffering and loss they have never even imagined in their own lives. Sometimes guilt arises over more concrete matters, too. A teacher might have important personal plans that cannot be rearranged to attend the funeral of a student, which makes him or her feel guilty about missing it.

Whatever the reason, the response is much the same as that for feelings of resentment—recognize that these are common reactions, set them aside while providing direct support to students, and seek further assistance if the feelings continue.

Coping with Guilt

Guilt can be complicated. When it is an ongoing theme in a person's life, counseling may be helpful. For the kind of guilt that comes and goes in everyday lives, the following steps can be helpful:

1. *Think about what happened.* What is the situation? Was someone hurt or disappointed? Were there better choices that could have been made? If so, what do you think they were?

2. *Think about responsibility.* Is the responsibility for this hurt genuinely yours? Is it shared with others? Was it or was it not a situation that was in your control?

3. *Do something differently.* Think about whether you can change something about the situation that would make it better. Could something be done that helps resolve or improve negative consequences from the situation? There might be something that indirectly makes the situation better. Then decide if you *want* to do any of these things.

4. *Ask forgiveness and make amends.* If you feel you've done something wrong, apologize to the person harmed.

5. *Let go and move on.* Once you have done what you can, or what you are willing to do, set aside the troublesome thoughts and focus on positive actions.

RECEIVING AND GIVING SUPPORT

One of the things teachers are asked to do with bereaved students is to encourage them to seek support from friends and adults they trust. Talking about the complex experiences of grief and loss is one of the best ways for children to work through their feelings and come to a meaningful personal understanding of a death.

This same strategy works for adults who are involved with bereaved children. Teachers, parents, health care providers, and mental health professionals all benefit from the opportunity to discuss their own responses to children's losses. Because witnessing the grief of a child can be an unsettling experience, it is important to identify friends, colleagues, and professionals who can listen well. It is also helpful to consciously plan personal strategies for managing stress, sadness, frustration, or other states that can interfere with work and personal life. The following are some suggestions:

- *Remember that grief is difficult.* These are painful feelings to experience and to witness. When grieving children—or adults—are asked to talk about the things they are feeling, they usually look distressed. They may become upset. They may cry or express anger or hopelessness. It is difficult to feel as if someone has been helped if he or she is obviously upset. If the person seems more distressed during or after the talk than prior to it, it might seem as if reaching out was unsuccessful. Yet, this very expression of painful feelings is what people most need to be able to do when they are grieving.

People often offer this kind of support at the point when the distress is greatest. If they do not have further discussions with the bereaved person, especially conversations about feelings, they may not see the signs of movement and recovery. This is an excellent reason to follow up with students a year or two later. Teachers will feel gratified and reassured when they see children doing better.

- *Talk with others.* Among family, friends, and colleagues, several people might be able to lend an ear. Simply telling the story (while respecting privacy issues) can sometimes lift the burden of sadness, discomfort, or concern. Even when teachers know rationally that they have been helpful to a student, that the reactions they are having are common, and that they have offered the type and amount of support that is appropriate for a teacher, it can help to hear someone they trust affirm this.

  It is also useful to look for something positive to share. Was a teacher struck by a surprising bit of wisdom from a student? Was the teacher gratified to know that a student trusted him or her? Was the teacher pleased to realize that he or she knew how to respond to a student's comments or questions? Adding in a positive observation makes the sharing easier on the listener. More important, it helps bring greater balance to the situation.

- *Talk with professionals.* There are times when the support of family, friends, and colleagues is not the right match for one's concerns, or it is simply not enough support. This is usually the case when discomfort, guilt, resentment, personal mourning, or other troublesome feelings persist, become especially strong, or interfere in some way with personal or work life. Talking with a mental health professional is also an important step when teachers are unsure about what to do for a grieving student, a family, or a class coping in some way with death. Professional help might come in the form of an employee assistance program, a mental health or bereavement specialist who acts as a consultant to the school or district, or a private therapist.

- *Build skills in stress management.* Teaching can be a stressful occupation, and having strategies for personal management of stress makes sense for all teachers. These skills can be particularly helpful for teachers when they offer support to bereaved students and come in a wide range of approaches. Some may work better than others. People have used simple exercises, such as deep breathing or muscle relaxation. Some find that regular physical activity and a healthy diet help them manage stress, feel better in general, and sleep better. Daily meditation, walks in nature, time with pets, and music are other approaches that are successful for some individuals.

  Courses and self-help books are also available that teach stress management exercises and skills. It is a good idea to identify several different approaches that work. Some can be used proactively (e.g., daily exercise), and others can be used when experiencing a particularly stressful day or moment. If one strategy does not work well in a given situation, another one might work better. Often, the approaches that work for managing stress are also good strategies for coping with other powerful feelings, such as sadness, frustration, anger, or anxiety.

- *Give support to others.* Other members of the school staff may also be helping bereaved students. Listening to them describe some of their own challenges is a generous and compassionate act, and it can be helpful personally. This may be an opportunity to learn from the modeling of others—perhaps a colleague uses an approach with students that other teachers have not thought of or tried. Often, someone else's experience provides a chance to work through a difficult situation vicariously. Thinking over what might be done in the same situation helps build skills in problem solving or provides a good way to answer a confusing question from a student.

    Finally, the simple act of helping others—in this case, by listening to their concerns—helps reinforce the positives in one's own life. People who have opportunities to connect with others and offer support generally experience greater overall satisfaction in their lives.

- *Seek consultation.* Teachers are much more likely to find it stressful to support a grieving student when they lack confidence in their skills in this area or are unsure of how to deal with the particular situation. Teachers should not hesitate to seek the advice of their school's mental health professional or another staff member who is particularly experienced in this area. They could also seek the help of a consultant outside the school. Receiving additional training helps build skills and confidence. In addition, reading this book, we hope, is an important step in that direction.

PREPARATION: READY TO HELP STUDENTS

The NCSCB strongly supports ongoing training for teachers on issues of death, grief, and bereavement. Training provides information, builds skills, and establishes norms about what teachers can and should do to support grieving children. One of the greatest benefits is that schools or districts that organize such trainings are making a clear administrative pronouncement that this type of support for students is appropriate, expected, and supported.

Trainings also allow a broader sharing of responsibility for the support of bereaved students. When more teachers understand and gain these skills, they can act with greater confidence. Students receive better support, and individual teachers are less likely to feel overwhelmed or resentful because they are carrying an unfair share of this work.

Because every grieving student's situation is unique, and because some students' situations are complicated, the NCSCB also encourages schools to establish an ongoing relationship with another professional who can provide consultation regarding issues that affect students who are grieving. This might be a school nurse or a health or mental health professional within the school district or in the community who is familiar with child development, mental health, and bereavement. Some communities have hospice programs with staff who specialize in bereavement among children and adolescents. Some cities have mental health, crisis, or bereavement programs affiliated with local medical or educational institutions.

Ideally, a consultant could help deliver staff trainings on children and grief. In addition to helping teachers and other staff learn about supporting bereaved students, this provides an opportunity to meet the consultant and make a connection. This will make it easier for teachers to contact the consultant at a future time with questions about specific situations they are facing.

TAKING CARE OF YOURSELF

Here is a simple truth about supporting children who are grieving: *If you are talking to children who have lost a family member or friend, or talking to students generally about death and grief, you will find yourself examining your own feelings about death.*

Students, through their own natural curiosity about the world, will offer all kinds of interesting ideas and questions. Because they can be quite sensitive to the feelings that accompany grief, teachers may see powerful expressions of emotion. Teachers will have reactions to their comments, questions, and feelings; their life experiences; and their families.

Teachers' life experiences will become part of this process. If they have lost loved ones in the past, they will probably revisit some of that grief. If a teacher has old, unresolved emotional issues with someone in his or her life who has died—a mother he or she did not get to say goodbye to, a brother who died after a painful family argument—those issues may well emerge again.

If someone in a teacher's life is dying, the teacher may feel his or her own anticipatory grief more keenly when talking with a bereaved student. As mentioned earlier, these are times when a teacher may have less to offer the grieving student and when it will be important to find others to step in.

Even if teachers have never known well anyone who died, they will come face-to-face with feelings and ideas about death. They might wonder if, when they do have this experience, they will cope as well as their students. They might struggle with how unfair it is that a child has to go through such a profound loss. They might feel anxious about the perfectly healthy loved ones in their own lives, because talking with children about death involves the recognition that life is fragile and uncertain—we and the people we love will also die one day.

Here, we think, is another truth about supporting grieving students: *You will be rewarded for doing it.* When we reflect on our conversations with children about death and grief, we find ourselves examining some of the most essential issues of our humanity. What is life? What is it about? What is it for? Why do people suffer? Many teachers find rewards in this sort of introspection.

These connections with students allow teachers to find meaning in their work and enrich their personal lives. If we never think about losing the people we care about, we may not be able to value our relationships as deeply. If we are overwhelmed by fears that those we love will die, we will find it difficult to enjoy the time we have in their company. However, when we find we are able to cope with these apprehensions, our acknowledgment that death is inevitable for everyone can actually enhance our lives.

Great literature, drama, movies, and art usually focus on issues of loss for good reasons. We are drawn into that experience for a period of time and then released, often with a deeper understanding of our own lives. Sharing in the experience of grief with children often has a similar effect.

This *is* emotional work. Taking steps to take care of oneself and support one's colleagues is an essential component of the work. By doing so, teachers will be able to offer the most useful support to their students. They will also get the most out of the process—personally and professionally.

Afterword

Support for the Present and the Future

Teachers know they can play an influential role in the lives of their students. Most teachers go into the profession because they, too, were inspired and supported by teachers when they were young. They care about the welfare of children, and they believe in the power of education to transform lives and societies.

The death of a family member or friend is a common experience that most children will have before they complete their schooling. When teachers step in to help children cope, it can be a powerful intervention. On balance, it is an excellent investment of time and effort. Often, adding just a few extra moments to an already existing lesson or responding to an unplanned teachable moment gives students a chance to understand more about common reactions to grief or the Four Concepts About Death—anticipatory guidance that will serve them well at whatever point they might face the death of someone they know. When a death does occur in a student's life, it usually takes only a little bit of time for a teacher to relay his or her concern to the student. These brief interventions can be enormously meaningful. They may be some of the most important and enduring lessons any teacher will provide.

We think the following stories from teachers who have taken such steps say it best.

I teach sixth-grade science. A student in one of my classes lost her mother to illness. I wasn't sure how to be a support for her, but decided to go to the funeral and hoped that would be helpful.

Her family's culture was different from my own, so there were things going on at the graveside and the service that weren't familiar to me. I felt some awkwardness personally, but I just kept being there, being respectful, thinking about my student, wishing her the best. After the service, I went up to speak to her. She turned around and just hugged me, and really held on! We stood there holding each other for a couple of minutes. I kept saying things like "This must be so hard for you. And you're going to be okay. I know it's really hard."

I'm so glad I made that effort to be there and to speak to her. I knew it made a big difference to her, so I felt better about myself as a teacher and, frankly, as a human being. It was the right thing to do. And she continued to be very connected to me and to the class through the rest of the year.

One of my students lost her brother tragically in a car accident. He was very young. I didn't know the family personally, but I did go to the wake. My student seemed appreciative that I attended.

I hugged her at the wake and told her I was sorry. She was out of school the rest of the week, but returned the following Monday. I just let her know she could take her time making up the work she missed. She didn't really need the extra time. She had kept up with everything.

After this, she seemed as if she was trying to show everyone she was fine. She smiled more than I had seen her smile all year. I checked in with her occasionally and let her know she could talk with me if she wanted to. But she never did.

I hope she felt supported by the things I said and did. It's a little hard to know for sure, but I'm still glad I reached out to her.

I had a student last year whose father died. She was having a hard time coping with this loss. Her mother never allowed her to express her emotions about this. She kept insisting her daughter just "get over it."

Fortunately, our district social worker had set up a support group for bereaved students. She's someone who has a counseling degree, and she has been a wonderful resource for our students. I referred my student to the group. The meetings occurred once a week during the school day. This made quite a difference for the girl. It was important for her to have some place where she could experience and make sense of her grief, and the group made that possible for her.

I teach in our school's special education program. I have an eighth grader who has a reading disability but otherwise learns easily. She's good with people; a little street smart; and a vivacious, outgoing girl. Both teachers and students have always liked her.

Early this year, something changed dramatically. She was angry, she acted out, her classroom performance went way down. No one could figure out what had happened—she just took a dive. I pulled her from class one day and said, "What's going on here? You're not the same person."

She told me that her "granny" had lung cancer and was going to die. This was clearly very upsetting to my student, but just having the opportunity to talk about it seemed to make things a little better. I let her know we could talk again any time she wanted. Soon after this, her family arranged for her to move in with the grandmother to help with her care.

Then this girl had another backslide. She was angry again. She didn't pay attention in class. She got into a yelling fight with another girl.

So I talked to her again. She said she couldn't sleep. Every night when she went to bed, she worried that she was going to wake up in the morning and find her grandmother dead. I called in the mother for a family talk. I told her, "You know, this is a lot of responsibility to put on a 14-year-old." Her mom agreed, and so she moved in with the grandmother, too.

That really seemed to settle things down. The grandmother passed away a couple of weeks ago. I was supposed to go away that weekend, but I felt like I needed to be at the funeral, and I'm glad I was able to go.

The girl is making a good recovery. She's back in school, keeping up with her work, getting along with her classmates. When I checked in with her, she said, "I never knew that teachers cared." That was a pretty powerful line for me to hear.

I think if I had not talked to her, she would have continued to have problems and probably would have left our school. And really, all I did was tell her it was okay for her to feel sad and scared about this—anyone would in this situation. My own father died of lung cancer, so I felt like I understood a lot of what she was going through. I believe the whole experience was healing for both me and my student.

In the work we have done through the National Center for School Crisis and Bereavement, we have been repeatedly impressed with the power of teachers' concerns for their grieving students. We welcome you into this community of educators who have made the effort to serve this critical role for their students. We are sure your students will be better off because of it.

References

Adams, D., & Deveau, E. (1987). When a brother or sister is dying of cancer: The vulnerability of the adolescent sibling. *Death Studies, 11,* 279–295.

Chin, D., Schonfeld, D., O'Hare, L., Mayne, S., Salovey, P., Showalter, D., et al. (1998). Elementary school-age children's developmental understanding of the causes of cancer. *Journal of Developmental & Behavioral Pediatrics, 19*(6), 397–403.

Clunies-Ross, C., & Lansdown, R. (1988). Concepts of death, illness and isolation found in children with leukaemia. *Child: Care, Health and Development, 14,* 373–386.

Cold Spring School. (1998). *Let's do health.* New Haven, CT. Retrieved March 13, 2010, from http://info.med.yale.edu/ycc/kidsinfo/

Emswiler, M., & Emswiler, J. (2000). *Guiding your child through grief.* New York: Bantam Books.

Glazer, J., & Schonfeld, D.J. (2007). Life-limiting illness, palliative care, and bereavement. In A. Martin & F. Volkmar (Eds.), *Lewis' child and adolescent psychiatry: A comprehensive textbook* (4th ed., pp. 971–980). Philadelphia: Lippincott Williams & Wilkins.

Greenham, D., & Lohmann, R. (1982). Children facing death: Recurring patterns of adaptation. *Health & Social Work, 7*(2), 89–94.

Krell, R., & Rabkin, L. (1979). The effects of sibling death on the surviving child: A family perspective. *Family Process, 18*(4), 471–477.

Kübler-Ross, E. (1969). *On death and dying.* New York: Scribner.

Leash, R. (1994). *Death notification: A practical guide to the process.* Hinesburg, VT: Upper Access.

National Center for School Crisis and Bereavement. (2006). *Guidelines for responding to the death of a student or school staff.* Retrieved March 23, 2010, from http://www.cincinnatichildrens.org/svc/alpha/s/school-crisis/guidelines-bereavement.htm

Osterweis, M., Solomon, F., & Green, M. (Eds.). (1984). *Bereavement: Reactions, consequences, and care.* Washington, DC: National Academies Press.

Rando, T. (1993). *Treatment of complicated mourning.* Champaign, IL: Research Press.

Schonfeld, D.J. (1993). Talking with children about death. *Journal of Pediatric Health Care 7,* 269–274.

Schonfeld, D.J. (1996). Talking with elementary school-age children about AIDS and death: Principles and guidelines for school nurses. *Journal of School Nursing, 12*(1), 26–32.

Schonfeld, D.J. (2002). Almost one year later: Looking back and looking ahead. *Journal of Developmental & Behavioral Pediatrics, 23*(4), 1–3.

Schonfeld, D.J (2005). Helping children deal with terrorism. In L. Osborn, T. DeWitt, L. First, & J. Zenel. (Eds.), *Pediatrics* (pp. 1600–1602). Philadelphia: Elsevier Mosby.

Schonfeld, D. (2007). Coping with the death of a student or staff member. *ERCMExpress,* 3(2), 1–12. (This article is available at http://ercm.ed.gov/views/documents/CopingW_Death_StudentOrStaff.pdf)

Schonfeld, D., Johnson, S., Perrin, E., O'Hare, L., & Cicchetti, D. (1993). Understanding of Acquired Immunodeficiency Syndrome by elementary school children—A developmental survey. *Pediatrics, 92*(3), 389–395.

Schonfeld, D., & Kappelman, M. (1990). The impact of school-based education on the young child's understanding of death. *Journal of Development & Behavioral Pediatrics, 11*(5), 247–252.

Schonfeld, D., Kline, M., & Members of the Crisis Intervention Committee. (1994). School-based crisis intervention: An organizational model. *Crisis Intervention and Time-Limited Treatment, 1*(2), 155–166.

Schonfeld, D., & Lewis, M. (2005). Dying children. In S. Parker, B. Zuckerman, & M. Augustyn (Eds.), *Developmental and behavioral pediatrics: A handbook for primary care* (2nd ed.; pp. 396–400). Philadelphia: Lippincott Williams & Wilkins.

Schonfeld, D., Lichtenstein, R., Kline, M., & Speese-Linehan, D. (2002). *How to prepare for and respond to a crisis.* (2nd ed.). Alexandria, VA: ASCD.

Schonfeld, D., & Newgass, S. (2003, September). School crisis response initiative. *OVC Bulletin.* U.S. Department of Justice, Office of Justice Programs (NCJ 197832). http://www.ojp.usdoj.gov/ovc/publications/bulletins/schoolcrisis/ncj197832.pdf.

Schonfeld, D., & Quackenbush, M. (2009). *After a loved one dies: How children grieve and how parents and other adults can support them.* New York: New York Life Foundation. (This resource can be downloaded for free or ordered in hardcopy for the cost of shipping and handling at http://www.nylgriefguide.com/exchange_default.asp)

Schonfeld, D., & Smilansky, S. (1989). A cross-cultural comparison of Israeli and American children's death concepts. *Death Studies, 13,* 593–604.

Schreiber, M., Gurwitch, R., & Wong, M. (2006). *Listen, protect, and connect—Model & teach: Psychological first aid (PFA) for students and teachers.* (This document can be freely downloaded from the Ready.Gov web site at http://www.ready.gov/kids/_downloads/PFA_SchoolCrisis.pdf)

Smilansky, S. (1987). *On death: Helping children understand and cope.* New York: Peter Lang Publishing.

Speece, M., & Brent, S. (1984). Children's understanding of death: A review of three components of a death concept. *Child Development, 55,* 1671–1686.

Spinetta, J. (1974). The dying child's awareness of death: A review. *Psychological Bulletin, 81,* 256–260.

Study Guide

This study guide is designed as an aid to self-study, as well as a tool for book or study groups. It can also be used by instructors and participants in workshops or courses. The study questions and activities will help readers reinforce their learning, understand the material more deeply, reflect on personal experiences that may influence their approach to bereaved children, and enhance the skills that will help them support students effectively.

This kind of study can also build stronger capabilities among a group of colleagues. Working together, they can establish an environment where students are provided anticipatory guidance about death and bereavement. With this learning, colleagues can support one another, students can better understand how to reach out to bereaved peers, and children experiencing bereavement will know they can turn to teachers and classmates for understanding and support.

For each chapter of the book, this guide includes questions and suggestions that cover the following:

- Key Concepts
- Self-Check questions that review key information
- Personal Reflections that address the learner's own experiences and attitudes and help identify unique strengths, as well as possible obstacles, to helping bereaved students
- Discussion Questions for groups that help participants learn from each other
- Practical Applications that encourage learners to identify areas in which they can actively apply some of their knowledge in their work with students

To keep the writing style simple, the questions in this Study Guide focus specifically on teachers in classroom settings. However, questions can easily be adapted for those who work in other settings, such as school counseling offices, district mental health services, school administration, or nonschool settings.

SUGGESTIONS FOR USING THIS GUIDE

Learners can use all or part of this guide in a variety of ways. The following are some suggestions:

- Review Key Concepts before and/or after reading a chapter.
- Review the Self-Check questions after reading a chapter to reinforce learning.

- Respond to one or more of the Personal Reflections questions in a journal.

- Facilitate a group discussion using the Discussion Questions.

- Take turns in a study group answering questions in one or more of the Self-Check, Personal Reflections, or Discussion Questions sections.

- Identify one or more steps you as an individual could take in the Practical Applications section, or discuss as a group which of these would be useful and appropriate in your setting.

- Talk informally with colleagues about the questions in the Personal Reflections or Discussion Questions sections.

- Share personal insights from your reading or the Personal Reflections sections with friends and family members.

INTRODUCTION: YES, THIS MATTERS

Key Concepts

- *Bereavement is common among children.* The experience of grief appears to be nearly universal among students. Before they reach adulthood, almost all children will experience the death of someone important to them.

- *Bereavement has an impact.* Bereavement can affect children's academic performance, mood, and social function.

- *Talking with children helps.* Supportive conversations between children and adults are immensely helpful to children.

- *Barriers to communicating about death and grief are numerous.* Children and adults often communicate differently about death and grief.

- *Children and teachers can learn skills.* These skills include understanding essential concepts about death, common reactions to bereavement, and effective ways to support bereaved individuals.

Self-Check

- What is known about the extent and impact of death and bereavement on children?

- What are common barriers to communication between adults and children about death and bereavement?

Personal Reflections

- What kinds of communications about death and bereavement have you seen in your work setting among adults? Among children? Between adults and children?

- Do you think of the topics of death and grief as fairly straightforward subjects to address with students, or do you find these more complex topics?

- Some teachers and school personnel feel this information is vital for their students, whereas others are not so certain. Where do you fall on this continuum? Think back on this reflection after you have read more of the book to see whether any of your perspectives have changed.

Discussion Questions

- What are some of the ways attention has already been paid to the issue of children and bereavement in your setting?

- After reading this introduction, do you believe there are ways your school or colleagues could bring more attention to this issue?

Practical Applications

- Be aware of any interactions among students in your setting addressing death and grief, whether serious or playful. Pay attention to your own reactions to the things students do and say in relation to these topics. Do these suggest anything to you about how easy or difficult it might be for you to address death and grief with children?

CHAPTER 1: WHY SCHOOLS AND TEACHERS? ISN'T THIS SOMEONES ELSE'S JOB?

Key Concepts

- *Children in general benefit by learning more about death and grief.* Anticipatory guidance, starting at the earliest grades, can help children cope better if they do experience a loss. This also prepares students to support peers who experience the death of a friend or family member.

- *Schools are an excellent setting for this learning.* Many features of schools can offer unique and powerful support to bereaved children.

- *Teachers play a unique role in these matters.* In most cases, teachers' distance from the death allows children to discuss their feelings and reactions without feeling a need to protect the teacher.

Self-Check

- What are some of the reasons schools are an excellent setting for children to learn more about death and grief?

- What are some of the ways teachers can provide support to grieving children that is distinct from that offered by family members?

- What are some of the strategies teachers can use to lay the groundwork to provide anticipatory guidance about death and grief for all students?

Personal Reflections

- Have you had an opportunity to talk with a class or individual students about death? What happened? How do you feel about the discussion that occurred? Do you feel the conversation was helpful to the student or students? If yes, in what ways? If no, what could have been done differently to make it more useful?

Discussion Question

- What are some of the ways in which learning about the concepts of death, the process of grief and bereavement, and ways to support others who are grieving could be integrated into regular coursework in your setting?

Practical Applications

- Look for teachable moments in classroom or group settings, or one-to-one with a student, where discussions of death or grief might be addressed. If you are not sure how to proceed, begin by simply looking for and identifying moments where such discussions would be possible. Later chapters will offer specific guidance.

CHAPTER 2: HOW CHILDREN UNDERSTAND DEATH

Key Concepts

- *Children and adults must understand the Four Concepts About Death to cope effectively with a personal loss.* These are

—Death is irreversible.

—All life functions end completely at the time of death.

—Everything that is alive eventually dies.

—Death is caused by physical reasons.

- *It is best not to assume what children know based on their age.* Most children understand these concepts by 5–7 years of age, but children who are much younger may also understand some or all of these concepts. Even adults, though, sometimes have problems accepting them in times of grief.

- *Children often have difficulty understanding adult explanations of death.* If they do not fully understand the concept, they may misunderstand what an adult is saying.

Self-Check

- What are some of the reasons children might not understand that death is irreversible?

- What are some of the common problems children have understanding death?

- How can families with religious beliefs about an afterlife respect those beliefs while helping children accurately understand the facts of a death?

- What are some of the ways infants and toddlers might experience the death of someone close to them?

- What are some of the ways adolescents might understand death differently from how younger children understand death? What are some of the ways adolescents' understanding might be similar to that of younger children?

- What are some of the points that teachers can keep in mind as they think about offering lessons about death, grief, strong emotions, and supporting friends?

Personal Reflections

- Have you ever experienced the types of miscommunications about death described in this chapter? If yes, what was the circumstance (e.g., as a child, you did not understand an explanation; as a parent, you found it difficult to communicate clearly with your child; as a teacher, a student did not understand something you were trying to communicate)? How did you feel about the experience?

- What is your own spiritual or religious perspective about death and the afterlife? Do the Four Concepts About Death fit comfortably with these perspectives?

- What are some of the ways your teaching helps children make sense of their world? Do the principles you apply in your everyday teaching cross over to teaching about death and grief in some way?

Discussion Questions

- What are some of the ways in which older children, teens, and adults might also struggle with the Four Concepts About Death?

- What are some of the trends in popular culture that are fashionable among your students that might interfere with these concepts about death (e.g., vampire stories, angels, horror movies, invulnerable superheroes)?

- What steps can you take to check your students' understanding of complex or challenging issues? How do you determine whether you and your students are understanding and communicating in different ways about a subject?

Practical Applications

- Notice elements in your own life or the lives of your students that challenge the Four Concepts About Death. For example, television shows or movies might show characters that go through experiences that logically should have resulted in death, such as jumping off a four-story building, but they continue to survive.

- Notice elements in your own or your students' lives that affirm the Four Concepts About Death. For example, children might have an opportunity to talk about missing a pet that has died, read a book or story where one of the characters dies or grieves the death of someone close, or participate in classes addressing these concepts about death.

CHAPTER 3: WHEN A DEATH OCCURS IN A CHILD'S LIFE

Key Concepts

- *Children grieve in individual ways, just as adults do.* Every student's situation is unique, and children's reactions will vary. So will the timeline for their bereavement.
- *Children may experience a range of emotions after a death.* These often include confusion, guilt, and anger.
- *A number of different factors affect the way children respond to a death.* These include differences in how children are as individuals, their coping skills, and the family situation.
- *It can be difficult to identify distress in grieving children.* Even children who appear to be doing well may be struggling with their feelings and in need of support.
- *Children who have experienced cumulative loss become more sensitized, not less, to these issues.* Children do not "get used to" death, even if they live in areas where death and violence are common.
- *In most situations, it is best if children are encouraged to attend funerals or memorials of a family member or close friend.* Children gain many benefits by being part of these events, and teachers may be able to guide families in making decisions that support their children.
- *Although every culture has a different approach to death, teachers can offer the best support by first becoming genuinely competent in their own culture.* Families are usually grateful when a caring teacher is able to ask how to be of help or offer support.

Self-Check

- What are some of the common reactions children may have to the death of a family member or friend?
- What are some reasons children might be reluctant to talk about a recent death with a teacher or family member?
- What are some of the ways guilt reactions after a death are different for young children and teens? Under what circumstances are guilt reactions more likely?
- What are some of the factors that typically affect how children adjust to the death of a loved one?

- What are some of the reasons teachers and parents might *underestimate* a child's reactions to death and need for support?
- What are the effects of cumulative loss on children?
- What are some of the ways families can help children prepare for a funeral or memorial and feel supported at the event? How is this knowledge helpful for teachers?

Personal Reflections

- Have any of your students experienced the death of a family member or close friend while you were their teacher? What happened? How did you learn of the death? How did your student respond?
- Have you seen a student become upset by discussions about a loved one who has died? What happened? How did you feel about the incident?
- What are some of your own culture's perspectives, attitudes, and practices about death? How are these different from those of your students or colleagues? What are some of the ways your own cultural perspectives can help you address death and bereavement with children and their families? Are there ways your own perspectives might create obstacles?

Discussion Questions

- What are some ways students in your setting might express thoughts or feelings about the death of a friend or family member? Consider both verbal and nonverbal styles of expression.
- What behaviors would you look for in children that would communicate their experience of grief? What differences do you see in the behaviors of younger children, older children, and adults in this regard?
- Some students live in neighborhoods where there is considerable violence and many deaths have occurred. Some have experienced communitywide events that have resulted in deaths (e.g., floods or other disasters). Others have had less experience of death in their community. How would you describe the background experience of your students and their community in relation to death and grief?
- What are some of the common cultural perspectives about death among your students' families? What are some of the things you have learned about the different ways individual families address death and grief?

Practical Applications

- Arrange an in-service or training for teachers in your setting that addresses children and funerals or memorials. The training can offer suggestions about how to guide families in making decisions about these events.

- Notice the ways children in your setting communicate about difficult feelings. These might include fear, anger, or grief. Many teachers are already familiar with these kinds of expressions. See if, by bringing special attention to this issue for a week or so, you become more aware of these communications or notice new things.

CHAPTER 4: SUPPORT FOR GRIEVING CHILDREN: WHAT TO DO

Key Concepts

- *There are steps schools and teachers can take that will help grieving children.* These include acknowledging the loss and communicating clearly and effectively with students and their families.

- *Grief is a painful process.* There is nothing anyone can do or say that will take away the pain or make the loss less powerful.

- *There are several goals in intervening with students.* These include decreasing isolation, increasing academic function, and helping children get support from family and friends.

- *It is important to understand how to be with grieving students.* Teachers will be more effective when they have a sense of what to say, how to act, and how to manage their own feelings about death and loss.

- *Communication is absolutely key to supporting grieving children and their families.* Teachers can use a range of strategies to open communication with students and families.

- *Addressing the Four Concepts About Death does not require discussions of religion.* These facts and principles do not conflict with different religious or cultural beliefs.

- *These interventions usually take a relatively short amount of time.* Once they understand the principles of these approaches, most teachers find it fairly easy to address such matters.

Self-Check

- Identify the main goals in intervening with grieving students.
- What are some ways to reach grieving children in a supportive and authentic manner?
- What are some things *not* to say to grieving children and families?
- What are some effective ways to be the kind of teacher students will talk with about grief and loss? How does one "invite the conversation"?
- What are some of the challenges and obstacles that can make it more difficult for students to talk with teachers about death and grief?

- What are some practical guidelines teachers can use to talk honestly about the facts of death and grief without moving into discussions of religion?
- What guidelines will help teachers address concerns that talking with students about death and grief will be too time consuming?

Personal Reflections

- Have students, friends, or family members talked to you about the death of someone they cared for? What was this like for you? Were you comfortable with the conversation? Did you feel uncertain about what to say at times?
- Have you ever spoken to someone about the death of someone close to you when the person said something awkward or unhelpful? What happened? Does this give you better ideas about how you can talk with others going through similar experiences?
- Do your students think you are approachable? Do they talk to you about important matters or personal issues? If yes, what are the things you do that help them feel comfortable with you? If no, what are some steps you could take to become more accessible?

Discussion Questions

- What are some effective ways to let students know you are available to talk with them about difficult topics such as death and grief? What approaches are likely to work best in your setting?
- What are some ways you have seen colleagues reach out effectively to students? What techniques do they use?
- What are the guidelines in your setting about discussion of religious issues? What steps can you take to address the Four Concepts About Death and other factual matters, listen to students' concerns, and support them emotionally while *not* violating any guidelines about discussions of religion?
- Do you feel that these efforts can be efficient as well as effective? Can you reach bereaved students in a meaningful way and still manage all of the demands of your role as an educator? How helpful are the guidelines in this chapter for managing these kinds of concerns?

Practical Applications

- Grieving students feel more comfortable approaching teachers who have talked about death, grief, or other difficult topics in the past. Find a way to bring up death or grief in a classroom situation, small group discussion, or one-to-one conversation with a student in the next week.
- Identify three of the skills listed in the section Communication Challenges and practice each one at least once in the coming week (e.g., asking one or two

open-ended questions about a personal experience, asking a student where he or she turns for emotional support, approaching a student in a common area and starting up a brief conversation). This can be on any topic. It does not need to focus on death, grief, or other serious matters.

CHAPTER 5: COMMUNICATION: WAYS TO MAKE CONTACT AND KEEP IT GOING

Key Concepts

- *Some people have a natural comfort level in talking about difficult issues, but many find it challenging.* Teachers who feel unsure about addressing grief with students can learn skills that will help them be effective.

- *Techniques for supporting bereaved students work across a range of circumstances and personality types.* In both complicated situations and those that are more straightforward, teachers can take steps that help.

- *It is common for grieving children to experience challenges in their schoolwork.* Many children experience difficulty concentrating, easy distractibility, awkwardness with peers, or loss of interest in schoolwork.

- *It is appropriate for teachers to make accommodations in assignments and tests for grieving students.* For example, a student might take on simpler assignments, do a paper instead of a test, or receive an extension on a due date.

Self-Check

- What are the steps that help teachers set a positive foundation when making contact with grieving children?

- Describe some statements that teachers could say to a student who has recently experienced the death of a family member or close friend.

- Describe some open-ended questions that teachers can use to keep communication with a student going.

- What are some of the accommodations that teachers can make for grieving students in their academic work?

- What are some steps that teachers can take to set limits if a grieving student expresses anger, says things that are hurtful to other students, or misbehaves in other ways?

Personal Reflections

- Do you feel like you are one of the people who is naturally comfortable talking about difficult issues or someone who has to put more effort into these endeavors?

- Have you made accommodations in assignments or tests for grieving students or students facing other hardships? If so, what have you done? How did it work? Do you feel your approach helped the student get back on track academically?

If you have not done this, do you think you would do so for a grieving student? Do you have any concerns about making these kinds of accommodations? If so, what are they?

• Has a student ever asked you a philosophical question that was challenging (e.g., Why do people have to die? What is the purpose of our lives? Why do terrible things happen in the world?)? How did you respond? How do you feel about the response you gave? If you were answering the question again, would you answer in a similar fashion or would you change your answer in some way?

Discussion Questions

• What are some ways school staff can support each other in their efforts to reach out to children who are grieving?

• Imagine that you and your colleagues are going to share observations and perspectives about a grieving student to determine the best strategies for offering support. What sorts of comments are most likely to be helpful?

• What sort of "safe space" arrangements could be made for students in your setting? Take into account your students' ages, the physical setting, school rules, and available resources.

• What are appropriate accommodations for teachers to make in a student's coursework after the death of a family member or friend? Do you think some students would handle such accommodations better than others? For example, would an academically gifted student need such accommodations less than a student with prior academic problems? Would it be easier to monitor these accommodations with a student you knew well and had a good relationship with than a student with whom you had not connected well?

• What approaches to *compassionate limit setting* have worked for you or for other teachers in your setting?

Practical Applications

• Work with your school to establish "safe space" arrangements and guidelines for children coping with the death of a family member or close friend. This might include identifying a location at the school that would work for this purpose, policies about student use of the space, identifying an adult who could be called upon to speak with a student if necessary, or other details.

• Think about the current coursework your students are pursuing. What are some accommodations that would make sense if one of your students experienced the death of a family member or friend?

• As a way to practice, use some of the approaches described in this chapter to keep social conversations going in the coming week. For example, you might ask family members or friends an open-ended question about how they are feeling or about something they have experienced. Then you could continue to ask a few open-ended questions to keep the conversation flowing. Focus more on listening and less on talking for a period of time to see how these techniques work.

CHAPTER 6: WORKING WITH FAMILIES

Key Concepts

- *Teachers and schools also play a special role with families.* They are a familiar and trusted resource, and grieving families often look to their children's teacher for support.

- *Teachers' observations and suggestions can be helpful for parents.* They can reinforce the importance of parents' roles, describe common reactions children have to a death, and share specific observations about how their children are doing with peers or in schoolwork.

- *Specific guidance is often important for families.* For example, they may appreciate learning about the Four Concepts About Death, the importance of being honest with children, or how to support their children in building an appropriate and useful understanding of death.

Self-Check

- What are some of the reasons teachers play an important and unique role for grieving families?

- What are some points teachers can discuss with parents that will help them provide the best possible support to their children?

- What are some reasons parents may not be able to provide appropriate support to their children after the death of a family member or close friend?

Personal Reflections

- Have you ever had a meeting with a parent that provided a "window into the family"—offering information that helped you better understand a student's situation or behavior? What happened? How did this help you be a better teacher for your student?

- Have you met with parents who did not seem to have their children's best interests at heart, or who did not know how to address their children's needs? Think about one instance that you remember. What happened? What did you say to the parents? Are there things you *didn't* say but think might have been helpful?

- Have you dealt with a family that was not able to provide appropriate support to a child after a death? What happened? How did you feel about it?

Discussion Questions

- What strategies for family contact are typically used in your setting? Which of these do you use?

- What skills for making contact with families are different from those you use to make contact with students? What skills are similar for both parents and children?

- When do you feel comfortable giving direct advice to parents about what they should say to or do with their children? When is it best to reflect these kinds of questions back to the parents?

- What points about children's understanding of death and how to support their grief do you feel are most important for families to understand?

Practical Applications

- Think about the "invitation" you have offered to families to contact you if they have concerns about their child. Is it your impression that they feel comfortable making contact? Is there more you think you could or should do? Are there things at the schoolwide level that would encourage greater family involvement?

CHAPTER 7:
SPECIAL CONCERNS
FOR BEREAVED CHILDREN

Key Concepts

- *For some people the process of grief is more complicated than usual.* This is sometimes called *complicated mourning.*

- *The degree of reactions and persistence of grief are key features of complicated mourning.* Whereas most people begin to feel a sense of positive movement after a few weeks or months, those with complicated grief may find their ability to cope becomes worse instead of better.

- *Children may experience complicated mourning themselves, or they may have a parent who is experiencing complicated mourning.* Both circumstances present immense challenges to children.

- *There are some situations where complicated mourning is more likely.* This includes times when there is something especially troubling about the death or when there are challenges in the student's family situation.

- *Children often experience secondary loss after the death of a family member.* This might include changes in living circumstances, finances, or social situations.

- *Children are more vulnerable to emotional and behavioral problems related to grief at times of transition.* This might include changing schools, moving, or experiencing a change in family constellation.

- *Students with special needs around learning and understanding may have addi-tional challenges coping with the death of a family member or close friend.* These students may need more attention and help understanding and coming to terms with the loss.

- *Children experiencing complicated mourning usually benefit from assistance from professionals.* Teachers play an important role in helping students gain access to this kind of help.

Self-Check

- What are some of the hallmarks of complicated mourning?

- Children experiencing complicated mourning often show typical symptoms of depression. What are some of these symptoms?

- What are some of the circumstances of the death that might increase the risk of complicated mourning?

- What are some of the characteristics of a student or his or her family that might increase the risk of complicated mourning?

- Describe some of the secondary losses that children might experience after the death of a family member.

- What are some of the ways teachers might be able to offer extra support to special education students after the death of a family member?

- What are some signs that a bereaved child might benefit from additional pro-fessional support?

Personal Reflections

- Have you ever known someone who experienced complicated mourning? What happened? How close were you to the person? How did you feel about it?

- If you have experienced the deaths of loved ones in your own life, how did the circumstances of the deaths affect you? For example, were your feelings different if a death was sudden, came after a long illness, or occurred to someone young?

- What are some secondary losses you have experienced in your own life, either through the death of a family member or other situations (e.g., loss of a job, not being accepted to a preferred college, loss of a relationship, illness or disability)?

Discussion Questions

- What role should teachers play in situations in which a student is experienc-ing complicated mourning or has a parent who is experiencing complicated mourning? What are reasonable steps for teachers to take in trying to arrange professional help for a student?

- What resources are available for students in your school who might be facing this type of situation?
- What are some things teachers can do if they see students respond in a negative or unsupportive way to deaths (e.g., teasing a surviving family member, making crude jokes in class)?

Practical Applications

- Identify resources for students in your school experiencing either typical or complicated mourning. Who can assess students' situations? How quickly can a student in need receive a referral and begin receiving support?
- Arrange a training that helps teachers identify signs of complicated mourning in students and describes how teachers can arrange appropriate assessment and referral for professional help.

CHAPTER 8: PROVIDING SUPPORT OVER TIME

Key Concepts

- *Grief changes over time.* Although there is no set timeline, most bereaved children and adults will experience reductions in the intensity and intrusiveness of their grief.
- *Grief affects many different domains in life.* Feelings, thoughts, and relationships at school or at home may be affected.
- *Anniversaries, transitions, special events, and rites of passage may all lead individuals to reexperience their grief.* At notable times such as these, children and adults often feel their loss more deeply.
- *A number of events or objects can act as triggers for grief.* These may catch people off guard and can be troubling to children.
- *Teachers can take a number of steps when they introduce activities or subjects that might be difficult for children who have experienced the death of someone close.* Being proactive in this way helps reassure all students while supporting those remembering a death.
- *Bereavement can last a lifetime.* Children who have lost a parent or sibling are especially likely to continue to be affected by the death and experience their grief in some way at each new stage in their lives.

Self-Check

- Describe some of the situations that commonly lead to reexperiences of grief.
- Describe common triggers of grief. Which ones are most likely to occur in the school setting?

- What are some of the steps teachers can take to introduce activities or subjects that might be difficult for bereaved children?

- What are some of the issues that may come up for bereaved students during school or other life transitions?

Personal Reflections

- Have you ever experienced a grief trigger? What happened? What was this like for you? How does this experience help you better understand how one of your students might feel in a similar situation?

- Have you ever changed the way you presented a lesson or activity because you knew or suspected one of your students had experienced the death of someone close? If so, what did you do? Are you satisfied today with the choices you made, or would you do something differently if you had the chance to do it over?

- What sorts of discussions about death have occurred in your classes? What, if any, personal feelings did these discussions raise for you? In what ways have these experiences influenced how you would approach similar discussions today?

Discussion Questions

- What are some ways a student experiencing a grief trigger might receive support in your setting? How would teachers know that a student was going through such an experience?

- What are some of the activities in your classroom or school that might be difficult for children who have experienced the death of a family member or friend? What are some effective ways you and other teachers can stay sensitive to those children's needs?

- Describe a national event that has involved death that occurred during your teaching career. Name the event and then describe the impact it had on your students. What impact did it have on teachers and other staff? What steps were taken to help students understand and make sense of the event?

Practical Applications

- Think about the way you introduce and teach subjects that involve death in some way. Identify three things you might do in addition to or instead of what you currently do that could make these lessons more helpful and positive for bereaved students.

- Arrange a training for colleagues that addresses how grief changes over time, how to respond to grief triggers, how to adapt lessons or discussions in sensitive ways, and how to support students during transitions.

CHAPTER 9: WHEN AN ENTIRE SCHOOL IS AFFECTED

Key Concepts

- *The death of a student, teacher, or other staff member can have a profound impact on the entire school.* Often, virtually everyone will have some sort of emotional response to the death.

- *It is important for schools to set up a system that offers students and staff support at such times.* This includes the services of school staff and/or consultants who have experience and skills in providing support during such crises.

- *Particular issues should be considered in school settings in which many people are sharing a grief experience at the same time.* For example, responses may be more intense, people may feel anxious, and rumors may spread quickly.

- *Steps similar to those that support individual students experiencing grief will be helpful when a group experiences a death.* Teachers can make a meaningful difference by establishing an authentic, supportive connection with students.

- *It is important for schools and teachers to reach out to students at higher risk for emotional distress after a school death.* This includes close friends of the deceased, classmates, and others who had some special connection to the person.

- *Deaths by suicide or homicide raise special concerns.* These include taking steps to prevent other students from harming themselves or others.

Self-Check

- What are the goals of support for students after a death has occurred in the school community? For staff?

- What are some of the common steps that are outlined in school crisis response plans that address the death of a member of the school community? Explain why it is important that these steps take place and that they occur in a particular sequence.

- It is important that all students receive information about a death in the school community. What are some of the special circumstances schools might need to consider to make sure that all students are informed?

- What are some common reactions in schools when the experience of grief is shared as a group?

- What are some steps teachers can take to offer support to students when grief is being experienced and expressed at the school level?
- Which students have a higher risk for emotional distress after a school death?
- What are the important steps for schools to take after the suicide of a student?

Personal Reflections

- Have you experienced the death of a student or colleague in your school? How deeply was the death experienced by students? By staff? By you, personally? How did you feel about the school's response to the incident (e.g., was it sufficient, helpful, appropriate, well-organized, or problematic?)?
- If you have experienced a death within your school community, what was that like for you emotionally? How did it feel to balance your role as a teacher with any emotional response you had to the death?

Discussion Questions

- What are the most important steps you can take in your role(s) at school (e.g., teacher, advisor, mentor) to provide support and understanding to students in the event of a death in the school community?
- What steps can be taken in your setting to reach out to and support students at higher risk for emotional distress after a school death?
- What are some of the challenges your school would face in the event of a student or staff member's death? (Or, what are some of the challenges your school *has* faced if such a death has already occurred?)

Practical Applications

- Review your school's guidelines for a death within the school community. After reading this chapter, do you see any additional steps that might be included in your school's guidelines? If so, are there ways you can encourage your school's crisis response team to update their guidelines?
- Identify the areas in this chapter where you feel best prepared to act and support students and the areas where you feel least prepared. Make a commitment to study the areas where your preparedness is weaker so that you are able to act with greater confidence should a death occur.

CHAPTER 10: SERIOUSLY ILL STUDENTS: WHEN DEATH IS A CONCERN

Key Concepts

- *Medical advances have made it possible for children with serious medical conditions to live longer and participate in school more fully.* It is not unusual for students at a terminal stage of illness to be in the classroom until very close to the time of death.

- *Teachers can take certain steps to provide support to such students and their families.* These include communicating honestly, helping the child have positive interactions with classmates, and working with the child and family to determine what information should be shared with classmates and their families.

- *There are also steps teachers can take to support the classmates of seriously or terminally ill children.* These include helping students understand more about the illness and its treatment, as well as how to receive support for oneself and provide support to others.

Self-Check

- Describe and explain the terms used in this book for children who are ill.

- What are some of the different understandings terminally ill children might have about death?

- What are some of the questions and concerns terminally ill children often have about their situation?

- Describe some of the different ways terminally ill children might want to share information about their condition with classmates.

- What are some of the needs of siblings of a seriously ill child, and how can these be addressed by teachers and schools?

Personal Reflections

- Have you ever had a seriously or terminally ill student in a class? What was this like for you? For the other students?

- How do you feel about the presence of such students in the classroom?

Discussion Questions

- What are some of the benefits of having seriously ill children take part in regular classes? What are some challenges for children who are ill? Their classmates? Their teachers?

- What can schools and teachers do to make the experiences of both ill children and their classmates positive and productive?

- How can schools best work with the families of seriously ill children? Whose responsibility is it to establish and maintain contact with families?

Practical Applications

- Has your school had seriously or terminally ill students in classes? After reading this chapter, can you identify anything your colleagues or administration might do differently in such situations? If so, can you take your recommendations to an individual or group that will take them into consideration?

- Can you identify anything you might do personally to make such situations more productive in your own classes?

CHAPTER 11:
MEMORIALIZATION AND COMMEMORATION

Key Concepts

- *Commemorations and memorializations help provide a context in which survivors can begin to make sense of a death.* They may find meaning and purpose in the life of the person who died.

- *Commemorations and memorializations can be helpful to children and are appropriate in school settings when a death has affected a classroom or school.* Simple activities are often all that is needed.

- *It is vital that students have a role in planning how to commemorate a classmate, teacher, or other member of the school community who has died.* Children can suggest activities that are relevant to their circumstances.

- *Teachers and schools can take steps to ensure that students plan a positive activity that makes sense to them.* These include asking questions, engaging them in discussion, exploring feelings, and helping them find direction.

- *Policies about memorialization can help schools plan appropriate activities that are most likely to benefit students and staff.*

Self-Check

- What are some of the reasons it is important to give students a role in planning commemoration and memorialization in a school setting?

- What are some questions teachers can ask students to help them plan a positive activity?

- What are some of the hallmarks of a positive commemorative activity?

- What are some of the challenges schools might face in planning and managing commemoration and memorialization?

- Describe some of the guidelines for recognizing and remembering students or staff who have died, and explain why these are appropriate guidelines for schools.

- What are some of the challenges with spontaneous memorials? How can schools address these challenges while allowing students opportunities for expression?

- What considerations do schools need to make when addressing the timing of commemoration and memorialization?

Personal Reflections

- Can you think of a commemoration or memorialization of someone you knew that had meaning and significance for you? (This does not have to be in a school setting.) What was it? Why did this approach have meaning for you?

- What features do you think would make memorialization meaningful for the kinds of students you teach? What would you hope students would gain by participating in such an event?

- Have you experienced memorializations in your school? If yes, do you feel they have been positive and productive, or have there been problems with the events? You might think about both formal and spontaneous or informal memorializations.

Discussion Questions

- What kinds of commemorative and memorial activities or events do you think would be—or have been—most useful for students in your school?

- In your setting, what would be the best way to give students a voice in planning commemorations and memorializations should a death occur?

- Are there any challenges in commemoration or memorialization that might arise—or have already come up—in your school that were not addressed in this chapter? If so, what are they?

Practical Applications

- Identify and review any policies your school has for recognizing and remembering students or staff who have died. After reading this chapter, do you see any additional elements that might be included in your school's policies? If so, are there ways you can encourage your school to update their policies?

- Are there policies or precedents at your school that ensure that students will have a voice in planning commemorative activities and memorialization? If not, is there any individual or group you can talk to about the importance of this opportunity for students?

CHAPTER 12: TAKING CARE OF YOURSELF

Key Concepts

- *Teachers gain benefits from offering anticipatory guidance to all students and support to bereaved students.* They touch their students' lives in powerful and meaningful ways, and this is very uplifting for most teachers.

- *Teachers may also feel apprehensive about taking these steps.* Teachers may feel unprepared to address matters related to death and grief, worry that they will say the wrong thing, or feel overextended and unable to offer the extra effort.

- *Teachers have a range of common reactions to these efforts.* These include such things as experiencing grief triggers, worrying about the support students get from their families, or being uncomfortable talking about death.
- *It is important for teachers to think about and plan ways to receive support from others when they are supporting bereaved students.* Talking with friends and colleagues about the complex experiences of grief and loss can help teachers manage many of the challenges of these efforts.
- *Witnessing the grief of a child can be an unsettling experience.* It is important to have friends and other adults to talk to about these things.
- *Teachers who talk with students about death and grief often find themselves examining their own feelings about death.* This can be both difficult and gratifying.

Self-Check

- Describe some of the common personal reactions teachers may have when they address death and grief with students.
- What are some of the reasons teachers might feel guilty about what they have chosen to do or felt unable to do to support bereaved students?
- What are some practical steps people can take to address feelings of guilt?
- What are some strategies that can help teachers manage stress, sadness, frustration, or other emotional states that may interfere with work and personal life?

Personal Reflections

- What feelings or memories do you have when you think about or observe a child experiencing grief? Without necessarily sharing them with the students, are there ways these personal experiences can help you be more effective with your students?
- What is something you find uncomfortable or challenging about addressing death and grief with students?
- Who do you turn to for support if you have emotional responses to your work with students (whether you are addressing death and grief or other issues)? How does this support help you?
- Who is someone who has been a model or mentor for you in addressing matters of death and grief or other complex issues facing students?

Discussion Questions

- What are the rewards of providing anticipatory guidance about death and grief or of reaching out to grieving students?
- What steps will help create a culture of support in your school for staff who are addressing issues of death and grief with students?

- What can teachers do to identify any personal limits they might have in supporting students coping with death and grief (e.g., feeling overextended or resentful, reexperiencing their own grief, feeling overinvolved with a student's situation)?

Practical Applications

- Reflect on the ways you address and manage stress in your life. Identify at least one new strategy to try in the coming week.

- Identify ways you can offer support to colleagues who are helping students understand death and grief. Find opportunities to practice some of these skills in the coming week, even if you do not have a colleague currently involved with a bereaved student. For example, listen to someone who is feeling challenged by a student's family situation, share resources about bereaved students with a colleague, or collaborate in developing a lesson plan that reviews the Four Concepts About Death.

- Find out if you have an employee assistance program in your work setting. If you do, share information about the program with other colleagues at your school.

Index

Page numbers followed by f indicate figures; those followed by t indicate tables; those followed by n indicate endnotes.